Clinical Guide to Music Therapy in Adult Physical Rehabilitation Settings

✦✦✦

Clinical Guide to Music Therapy in Adult Physical Rehabilitation Settings

♦♦♦

Elizabeth H. Wong, MT-BC

American Music Therapy Association, Inc.

Neither the American Music Therapy Association nor its Executive Board is responsible for the conclusions reached or the opinions expressed by the contributors to this book.

The American Music Therapy Association is a nonprofit association dedicated to increasing access to quality music therapy services for individuals with disabilities or illnesses or for those who are interested in personal growth and wellness. AMTA provides extensive educational and research information about the music therapy profession. Referrals for qualified music therapists are also provided to consumers and parents. AMTA holds an annual conference every autumn and its eight regions hold conferences every spring.

For up-to-date information, please access the AMTA website at www.musictherapy.org

ISBN: 9781884914119

The American Music Therapy Association, Inc.
8455 Colesville Road, Suite 1000
Silver Spring, MD 20910

Phone: (301) 589-3300
Fax: (301) 589-5175
Email: info@musictherapy.org
Website: www.musictherapy.org

Printed in The United States of America

ACKNOWLEDGMENTS

✦✦✦

There are a lot of people who helped me to write this book by answering my questions, taking time to explain concepts, and being supportive. I would like to personally thank Ann P. Gervin, MT-BC, for all of her time and guidance when I started. I would also like to thank Renee Fulford, CCC-SLP, Amy Reese, COTA, Michael Chappell, R.R.T, Scott Gill, R.R.T, and Kim Jordan, CCC-SLP for teaching me so much through the years. I would especially like to thank Fiona Byrne-Flores, CCC-SLP, for reading through the book and allowing me to pick her brain. I could not have written this book without you all. I would also like to thank Joe Holliday for the great illustrations, and Berta and James Holliday for all of your encouragement and guidance through the years. Most of all, I would like to thank my husband, Sam.

EDITORIAL CONSULTANTS:

Janice W. Stouffer, MT-BC
Music Therapist
Department of Orthopedics and Rehabilitation
Penn State Milton S. Hershey Medical Center
Hershey, Pennsylvania

David S. Smith, Ph.D., MT-BC
School of Music
Western Michigan University
Kalamazoo, Michigan

CONTENTS

✦✦✦

Contents, continued

FOREWORD

◆◆◆

When I landed a job at the adult rehabilitation hospital, I kept my eyes and ears open, asked questions, and took notes on every bit of information possible. By doing this, I was able to learn a great deal in a relatively short period of time, thanks to some very friendly, intelligent, and considerate co-workers and colleagues who were always willing to answer my questions or allow me to observe them in therapy. Most of the employees had never heard of music therapy.

This book was designed to "arm" the entry-level music therapist or an experienced MT-BC, new to the hospital setting, with the basic knowledge and materials to develop or continue a music therapy program in a rehabilitation setting with stroke, brain injury, and ventilator patients. In the physical rehabilitation treatment setting, target outcomes fall under two general categories: (1) improvement of functional skills, and (2) facilitation of psychosocial adjustment and emotional coping during hospitalization. Functional skills, those tasks that are found in the motor, cognitive, sensory, and communication domains, are traditionally addressed by physical, occupational, and speech therapists, as well as the music therapist. The tasks of emotional coping and the role these skills play in treatment are often overlooked or addressed partially by social work or a case manager in those facilities that do not have music therapy services. The goals and treatment suggestions presented in the following chapters are intended to encompass all of these vital target outcomes, thus assisting the music therapist in addressing the needs of the whole person.

It should be noted that the background information and activities presented are most appropriate to the adult rehabilitation population. Goals, techniques, and approaches would need to be modified developmentally for use with pediatrics.

Hopefully, the use of this book will facilitate the process of entering a new setting and will allow the music therapist to have some good nights' rest during the adjustment period. As with any new job, you're going to need them!

— Elizabeth H. Wong

CHAPTER 1

♦♦♦

CEREBROVASCULAR ACCIDENT

General Information

A cerebrovascular accident, or CVA, is commonly called a stroke. Strokes occur when arteries or veins burst or become clogged. As a result, parts of the brain do not receive the flow of blood they need. The lack of blood flow causes those areas of the brain to be damaged or even die.

Types and Characteristics

Ischemic

Ischemic strokes are the most common type of stroke., and are caused by a decreased blood supply. (Ischemia means a lack of blood flow and a decrease delivery of oxygen to the cells.) There are two causes of ischemic strokes: thrombus and embolus.

A thrombus is a clot in a blood vessel. It forms in arteries impaired by arteriosclerosis, a disease that causes the arterial walls to become lined with thick fatty deposits.

An embolus is a sudden blocking of an artery by a blood clot or other foreign matter. Such foreign particles often originate from diseased areas in the heart.

Hemorrhagic

A hemorrhage is a bleed. Hemorrhagic CVAs results from the rupture of a blood vessel in the brain which allows blood to cover the surrounding tissue. Blood directly touching the brain causes damage to the brain tissues. An aneurysm, or an enlarged, weakened blood vessel, that bursts causes a hemorrhagic stroke.

Usually a patient's medical chart will state exactly where the hemorrhage occurs. For instance, the chart may state that the person has had a subarachnoid hemorrhage. Thus, the bleed was in the subarachnoid space. Specific lobes that are damaged provide some insight into a patient's deficits: a person whose frontal lobe was damaged is likely to be impulsive and have poor reasoning and planning skills.

TIA: The "Mini Stroke"

A TIA stands for a transient ischemic attack., and are considered a sort of "mini-stroke." Many strokes are preceded by TIAs that may occur days, weeks, or months before a major stroke. Having a TIA increases a person's risk for having a stroke in the future.

A TIA occurs when a blood clot temporarily clogs a blood vessel and specific areas of the brain don't get the blood supply necessary to maintain function. The person experiences sudden but short-lived symptoms of a CVA, including:

- sudden decreased vision
- sudden weakness and/or numbness of the leg, arm, and face on one side of the body
- sudden, severe headache with no apparent cause
- decreased ability to speak, difficulty understanding speech
- unexplained dizziness or sudden falls, especially coupled with other symptoms

Brain Anatomy

As stated above, the specific location and the severity of the CVA determines the type of functional deficits and the severity of the deficits the patient might present. This sets the parameters and goals for the rehabilitative therapy. The following information will provide a quick neuroanatomy refresher course to make the rest of the chapter more comprehensible (also see Figure 1).

The brain consists of the brainstem, the cerebellum, and the cerebrum:

- *Brainstem* contains the basic functions such as blood pressure, heart rate, breathing, and staying alert (or arousal).

- *Cerebellum* controls movements and balance.

- *Cerebrum* regulates the higher-functioning thought, memory, and perception.

The cerebrum is divided into two hemispheres, the left and right. They communicate via the corpus callosum which runs between them.

Left Hemisphere
- language; speech, comprehension, reading, writing
- rhythm perception
- reasoning
- numerical skills

Right Hemisphere
- music, art, drawing, dancing, copying
- insight, problem solving
- visual memories
- imagination

There are four lobes in the brain: the frontal, parietal, temporal, and occipital.

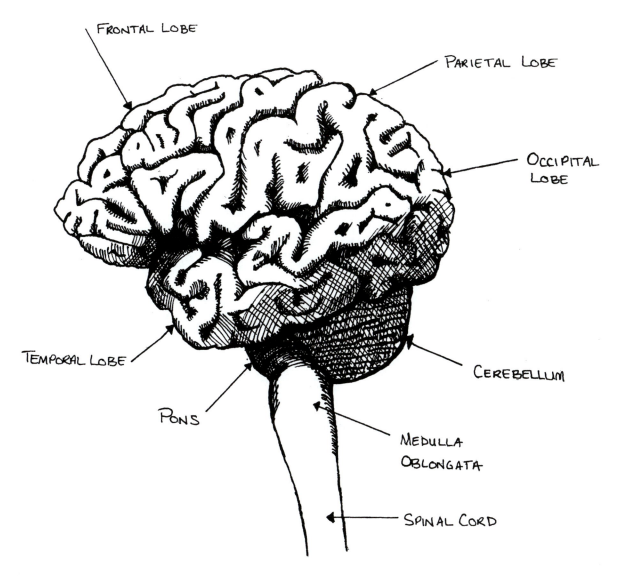

Figure 1. Labeled Drawing of the Brain

- *Frontal Lobe* is in the front of your head. It is responsible for motivation, impulse, initiation, planning, problem solving, attention, decision-making, social abilities, sense of smell, and creative thought.

- *Temporal Lobe* is located just behind and below the frontal lobe. It is responsible for memories, emotions, auditory sequencing, understanding language, and music appreciation.

- *Parietal Lobe* is found just above the temporal lobe. It controls academic abilities such as reading comprehension and spatial relationships. It also regulates tactile stimulation and recognition.

- *Occipital Lobe* is found in the very back of the head. It is responsible only for sight. Blindness can result from damage to the occipital lobe. This is sometimes referred to as occipital blindness.

Left-Brain Strokes Versus Right-Brain Strokes

Strokes affect only certain areas of the brain. Prior to the stroke, these areas were once responsible for a certain aspect of the patient's personality and abilities. After a CVA, those areas contain deficits.

A stroke in the left hemisphere will affect the right side of the body, and vice versa. Stroke patients are, of course, very different depending upon their injury, their premorbid personality, and how recently the stroke occurred. However, there are general characteristics of left stroke and right stroke patients.

Left-Brain Stroke
- right side of body affected
- aphasia/apraxia
- judgment, memory, attention span, relatively intact
- numerical skills

Right-Brain Stroke
- left side of body affected
- dysarthria/dysphagia
- left neglect
- impulsive
- decreased sensory awareness
- impaired memory/attention span
- poor insight
- poor judgment
- emotional lability

Quick reference guide to terms in chart:

aphasia: decreased ability to communicate.

apraxia: decreased muscle coordination to complete a task; inability to perform purposeful movements though no muscular weakness is present.

dysarthria: weakness in mouth, tongue, throat, and/or respiratory system, causing difficulty with speaking and eating.

dysphagia: swallowing deficits.

neglect: the condition of "forgetting" about one side. Not attending to the affected side.

insight: an emotional and cognitive understanding of a situation.

lability: quickly fluctuating to extremes emotionally; sudden, inappropriate laughing or crying for no apparent reason.

It is necessary to remember the above chart is only a guideline. In a small percentage of patients, a person will have a right stroke (with the left side affected) and still have aphasia. As with anything else, there are exceptions to the norm.

Some CVA patients may present like brain-injured patients and vice versa. In a technical sense, a stroke is an injury to the brain. Hence, the two populations will often have common goals due to the similarities in the neurological impairment.

Goals for Patients With Cerebrovascular Accidents

In a physical rehabilitation setting, your patients have most likely had a traumatic insult or accident and need a lot of attention. Due to cutbacks and a focus on cost-efficiency, insurance usually sends to an inpatient hospital those individuals who cannot care for themselves or need extra medical attention on a 24-hour basis, whether it is for a few days or a few weeks.

During this time, the primary goal is to help an individual patient become as independent and self-sufficient as possible. Therefore, the fundamental goals are to increase psychosocial and emotional adjustment, and to increase functional motor, cognitive, and communication skills. How do you do these things? By addressing each deficit. This book will help you do that.

Left-brain CVA goals include but are not limited to:

- Increase communication skills (see chapters on aphasia and apraxia)
- Increase upper extremity strength, coordination, and/or range of motion
- Increase lower extremity strength, coordination, and/or range of motion
- Increase static and dynamic sitting balance

Right Brain CVA goals include but are not limited to:

- Increase lip, tongue, and oral motor strength (see chapter on dysarthria)
- Increase social skills, pragmatics, turn-taking

- Increase attention to task and memory (see chapter on cognition)
- Increase judgment, insight, and safety awareness (see chapter on cognition)
- Increase attention to neglected side (see chapter on cognition)
- Increase problem-solving skills (see chapter on cognition)
- Increase orientation (see chapter on cognition)
- Multi-task activities (see chapter on cognition)
- Increase upper extremity strength, coordination, and/or range of motion
- Increase lower extremity strength, coordination, and/or range of motion
- Increase static and dynamic sitting balance

Because there is so much overlap among the various diagnoses, it is difficult to isolate a particular deficit to one area. For instance, a stroke patient, a brain injury patient, and a ventilator patient all may have decreased attention spans. A ventilator patient may be on the ventilator due to a severe brain injury acquired in an automobile accident. It may be necessary to reference several sections of this book for such a patient.

In the same way, specific activities may have a variety of purposes. For instance, playing the keyboard can be used to promote good sitting balance, increase fine motor dexterity, and it is cognitively a multi-task activity. Keep this concept in mind while reading this book.

CHAPTER 2

✦✦✦

TRAUMATIC BRAIN INJURY

General Information

Traumatic brain injury occurs when any traumatic event causes injury to the brain. Most traumatic brain injuries occur within the ages of 18-24 and are often caused by car accidents. Traumatic brain injuries occurring in adults over 70 years old are frequently caused by falls.

Types and Characteristics

Open Head Injury results when something passes through the skull, like a bullet. Open head injuries affect a specific area of the brain, so damage and deficits are usually more specific.

Closed Head Injury occurs when the brain is injured but the skull is not penetrated. It may be due to an impact, such as a baseball. A closed head injury (CHI) causes diffuse damage and therefore the person's functional deficits are more diverse.

Brain injuries frequently cause people to go into comas. Comas on television bear little resemblance to comas in real life. People do not just "wake up" and immediately remember everyone around them, maintain a normal conversation, or crack jokes. Comatose patients may open their eyes, vocalize, have gross motor movements, and still be considered "in a coma." Comatose patients require a lot of therapy and attention.

Researchers have devised different models to measure the depth of comas. Comas are difficult to research objectively because patients don't usually remember anything about them or their accidents. Often researchers simply test physiological responses, such as heart rate or blood pressure, and observable behaviors such as facial twitches or gross motor movements.

Coma Measurement Instruments

Two very popular tools used to measure comas are the *Glasgow Coma Scale*, often used in acute care facilities, and the *Ranchos Los Amigos Scale of Cognitive Functioning*, commonly used in the rehabilitation setting.

Glascow Coma Scale

The *Glasgow Coma Scale* (GCS) (Argyris, 1994) is a measurement used to depict the severity of the coma state by measuring the observable motor and eye movements and the verbal responses. The medical staff uses the scale as an evaluation tool upon admit, then continues to test in order to measure progress. The higher the score, the better the patient's prognosis. The GCS is scored on a scale of 3 to 15 points: 3-8 usually indicates a severe brain injury, 9-12 indicates a moderate brain injury, 13-15 indicates a mild brain injury. It is scored as following:

Eye Opening
1. The patient does not open eyes.
2. The patient opens eyes with the application of painful stimuli.
3. The patient opens eyes on command in a loud voice.
4. The patient opens eyes on his/her own.

Motor Responses
1. The patient has no movements, even to painful stimuli.
2. The patient's body automatically becomes rigid in an extended position when pain is applied.
3. The patient's body bends at the elbows and wrists automatically with painful stimuli.
4. The patient pulls part of the body away from painful pressure purposefully and appropriately.
5. The patient pushes examiner's hand away when painful stimuli is applied.
6. The patient follows simple commands and can move body parts as directed.

Verbal Responses
1. The patient makes no noises.
2. The patient vocalizes (i.e., grunting, etc.).
3. The patient talks unintelligibly or does not make sense.
4. The patient talks but is confused and disoriented.
5. The patient carries on a conversation intelligibly and is oriented to place, month, and year.

Painful stimuli includes "tests" such as a *sternum rub*, when you rub your knuckles along the patient's sternum, or putting pressure on the bone in the area where the eye and nose meet.

Another test of coma severity sometimes given is the *Western Neuro Sensory Stimulation Profile* (WNSSP) (Ansell, Keenan, de la Rocka, 1989). This not only measures eye, body, and verbal responses but measures the ability of the patient to follow verbal and written commands, name objects, and use common objects functionally such as a cup, a brush, etc.

Ranchos Los Amigos Scale of Cognitive Functioning

The Ranchos Los Amigos Medical Center in California began categorizing coma behaviors into a series of cognitive levels I through VIII to describe a patient's progress. Usually patients are in acute care through Level I or II. Then they are brought to a rehabilitation hospital and are discharged by Level V or VI. They may continue therapy at home, as an outpatient, or in a specialized facility. Of course, this is a gross generalization since situations vary greatly from case to case. Any patient's discharge depends upon their medical stability, significant progress made, physical independence, and insurance coverage.

The Ranchos Los Amigos Levels of Cognitive Functioning (Hagen, Malkmus, & Durham, 1972) are as follows:

Level I No Response
- Patient does not respond to any sensory stimulation.

Level II Generalized Response
- Patient begins to respond to stimulation inconsistently or with delay.
- Patient responds to stimulation in the same way, such as body movements, vocalizations, or physiological changes.

Level III Localized Response
- Patient is awake on and off during the day.
- Patient makes more movements, has some automatic responses.
- Patient reacts more specifically to stimuli, i.e. localizing to sound, attempting to watch a person walk around the room, etc.
- Patient reacts slowly and inconsistently.
- Patient follows some simple directions, slowly and inconsistently.
- Patient inconsistently answers yes and no.

Level IV Confused, Agitated
- Patient is confused and frightened.
- Patient may not understand what is happening.
- Patient may overreact to stimuli, often by hitting, screaming, swearing, crying, etc.
- Patient cannot attend to task for a few seconds.
- Patient has difficulty following directions.
- Patient recognizes family and friends inconsistently.
- Patient may be able to complete simple routine activities with assistance.

Level V Confused, Inappropriate, Non-Agitated
- Patient can attend to task for a few minutes.
- Patient is confused and disoriented.
- Patient is able to respond to simple directions consistently.
- Patient is highly distractible.
- Verbalizations are often inappropriate.
- Patient may *confabulate*, or say things that aren't true without intending to lie.
- Memory is severely impaired.
- Perseverations may be present.

Level VI Confused, Appropriate
- Patient has problem solving, judgment, and memory deficits.
- Patient may remember month and year.
- Responses may be incorrect due to memory problems; however, they are appropriate.
- Patient shows some goal-directed behavior.

Level VII Automatic, Appropriate
- Patient oriented to hospital setting, follows set schedule.
- Patient still has short term memory deficits.
- Patient has superficial awareness of deficits, but lacks insight as to the extent, the implications, etc.
- Patient lacks realistic planning abilities for future goals.

Level VIII Purposeful, Appropriate
- Patient is alert and oriented.
- Patient is aware and responsive to culture, past, and present events.
- Patient is independent and needs little or no supervision after learning a task.
- Patient may show increase of abstract reasoning and tolerance for stress in unusual circumstances.
- Patient may be self centered, argumentative, depressed.
- Patient is unable to recognize inappropriate social interaction or recognize a problem while it is occurring.

The following levels have been added to the scale in the past few years:

Level IX

- Patient is able to use assistive memory devices to recall daily schedule or lists.
- Patient initiates and carries out routine tasks without assistance and unusual tasks with minimal assistance.
- Patient is able to think about consequences of actions with assistance when requested.
- Patient may exhibit signs of depression, irritability, and have a low frustration tolerance.
- Patient is able to self monitor social interaction with stand-by assistance.

Level X

- Patient is able to handle multiple tasks simultaneously but may require periodic breaks.
- Patient accurately estimates abilities and independently adjusts to task demands.
- Patient's social behavior is consistently appropriate.
- Patient is periodically depressed, irritable, and tolerating minimal frustration, particularly during periods of stress

Although these levels are tremendously helpful in communicating to others the status of a patient as well as giving family members a glance at the road ahead, not all patients are alike. Some patients skip levels while others stay in a level for weeks or never progress to the next level. Progress from one level to the next is not guaranteed. This is very important for family members to realize when they are asking questions about prognosis.

Working With the Family

As with any other serious ailment, TBIs are very emotional and traumatic for the family, especially if the patient is a child or teenager. Some families pull together and work as a team. Other families fight among themselves and/or take their frustrations out on the hospital staff. Families of teenagers have a very difficult time adjusting to the situation and usually have many questions.

Family members not only will ask a lot of questions, but sometimes manipulative members will ask the same questions to different therapists and doctors. Some families are so upset they will try to manipulate or place blame on the staff for any reason. It is vital to document carefully when working with such a family. It is also necessary for all professionals to "stay on the same page." If one therapist paints a different picture or gives conflicting information, it only confuses matters. This will make a family distrust the facility and its employees. If you don't know the answer to a question, it's better to admit the truth and find the correct answer, or direct the family to someone who can answer the question accurately.

Family members often report that a comatose patient responds in a certain way before medical staff observes such a response. For example, they may say that their daughter Sheila squeezes her mother's hand and moves her left foot when her mother tells her to. Such a response may result because the patient recognizes and responds better to the familiar voices and faces. Many accounts suggest that patients may respond better to familiar stimuli, especially family members and friends. However, it is important to differentiate between purposeful movements and reflexes. While family members may observe behaviors that therapists may have not witnessed, they are not professionals. Some family members may be so anxious for the patient to improve that they may exaggerate or mistake a reflex as a purposeful movement or vocalization. For example, when patients with a "hemi arm" yawn, their weak arm usually moves upward or contracts. This looks like movement, but it is actually a reflex.

When treating a patient and reporting progress, it is important to keep the reports accurate. Stating "Sheila squeezes hands on command" may not be the most accurate report. "The mother states that Sheila squeezes her hand inconsistently on command" depicts a more exact view of the situation.

Hearing Screens

As soon as appropriate, many hospitals will conduct hearing screens to rule out any hearing impairment acquired during the accident or insult. Such information could be vital during coma stimulation. For instance, if a person is not responding, is it due to their lack of consciousness, or a hearing impairment that occurred during the accident?

There are two hearing screens commonly used: the Otoacoustic Emissions Test (OAE), and the Auditory Brainstem Response (ABR). The OAE can be used with infants, unconscious patients, and anyone else who cannot accurately respond verbally to hearing screens because it detects a physiological response. During the test, a stimulus, usually clicks or tones, are presented to the ear. Then a microphone records the outer hair cell movement in the cochlea in response to the stimulus. Otoacoustic emissions, or the movement responses, are present when outer hairs are healthy, which means little or no measurable hearing loss. The emissions are absent when hair cells are damaged, which means there is a greater than mild hearing loss. However, there could be several reasons for absent otoacoustic emissions, so further tests are usually administered to determine the exact diagnosis (Stach, 2002).

ABR tests how the brainstem responds to specific auditory stimuli. Electrodes placed on the patient's head measure the brainstem's responses to the stimuli. ABR can be useful in diagnosing and evaluating hearing loss, acoustic neuromas (or benign tumors), lesions of the eighth nerve and brainstem, brain death, and demyelinating diseases such as multiple sclerosis (Stach, 2002).

Coma Stimulation

Coma stimulation is a somewhat controversial topic in that it is difficult to measure the benefits empirically. The term simply refers to sensory stimulation while the patient is in a comatose state. Several articles have been written comparing and contrasting views on the merit of such practice (Bontke, 1992). Some doctors feel sensory stimulation is a waste of time simply because there are no proven benefits. Others feel there is no proof coma stimulation does *not* benefit patients.

Research regarding the subject has been somewhat contradictory as well. However, at least some research suggests that sensory stimulation positively affects the responsiveness of these patients (Bontke, 1992). More controversy arises when deciding how much stimulation and what kind of stimulation are most advantageous.

To the Music Therapist: Taking Data

Music therapy is a potentially powerful tool for auditory stimulation of patients in Levels I and II. Have the patient's family or friends bring music the patient listened to premorbidly. Choose a slow selection and tape 1-2 minutes of it. A slow selection can be defined as one with roughly 75 BPM or less, preferably no lyrics and no drum beat, and generally relaxing. This selection of music will hopefully provoke relaxed physiological responses.

Record the slow selection on to a cassette tape. Let the tape run for 1-2 minutes of silence, keeping in mind that these selections should all be the same timed interval; for example if you choose 1.5 minutes, the music intervals and silence intervals should all be consistently 1.5 minutes. Next choose a fast or upbeat selection, roughly 120 BPM, and tape 1-2 minutes of it. Follow with another interval of silence, then the same slow selection, silence, and the same fast selection.

Start with a baseline pulse, oxygen saturation reading, and motor movements such as fingers or facial muscles. Keep a record of any changes during each musical selection to provide observed, measured data regarding the impact of music on the comatose patient.

The recorded pattern of music allows a baseline reading of pulse, oxygen saturation, and observable motor movements, an intervention (the slow selection), return to baseline (silence), an intervention (fast selection), and so on. The key thing to look for is a trend in a physiological, motor, or verbal response to these selections, such as an increase in heart rate during the fast selections, and a decrease during the slow selections. This would indicate that the patient is reacting to the environment, and therefore may be more aware of the surroundings. Such an indication could detect a patient "waking up."

If a patient has cardiac precautions or already has a high baseline pulse, discuss with nursing or other appropriate staff the appropriateness of using a fast selection to increase the heart rate, blood pressure, etc. You may want to begin with a slow selection for such a patient or alter the program to fit specific needs. Use the worksheet provided (see Figure 2) as a starter and change the worksheet to fit your needs if necessary.

There are machines designed to measure oxygen saturation, pulse rate, and other physiological parameters which greatly facilitate the data recording process. Discuss with the nursing and the respiratory therapy staff to determine what machines are available to you and the procedures involved. For instance, does every patient with a trach have an oxygen saturation monitor and pulse oximeter? If not, how can you get one during your therapy sessions?

When playing the selections during your treatment time, have the patient wear a set of headphones connected to a Walkman while you wear another set connected to the same Walkman so there are no distractions from TVs, noisy machines, or other people talking in the hall. It is important, however, to be sure the volume on the headset is no greater than 80 db.

Working With the Patients

Appropriate or positive coma stimulation includes family members, friends, television, and music the patient listened to premorbidly. Stimulation should be at a low to moderate noise level. It is important to remember it is very easy to overstimulate the patient, therefore, basic guidelines should be followed:

- Stimulation should be given in timed increments throughout the day (allow the patient some peace and quiet throughout the day). Coordinate schedule with other therapies.
- Only one person should talk to the patient at a time.
- The number of people in the room at one time should be limited to two or three (including family members and visitors).
- Turn off the television and radio while talking to the patient or anyone else in the room.

PATIENT _____

MUSIC THERAPY COMA STIMULATION

DATES _____

Responses	Monday	Tuesday	Wednesday	Thursday	Friday
base pulse/O2 sat					
sed /stim					
silence pulse/O2 sat					
sed/stim					
silence pulse/O2 sat					
sed/ stim					
silence pulse/O2 sat					
sed /stim					
ending pulse/O2 sat					
other responses					

Visual Tracking
A. Tracks paper without music
B. Tracks paper with music
C. Tracks drum without music
D. Tracks drum with music

One Step Commands
A. Squeeze hand
B. Smile   F. Move leg (R) or (L)
C. Open eyes   G. Look at me
D. Close eyes
E. Wiggle fingers

0=No response
1=eyes open
2=eyes closed
3=moves head
4=moves UE (R or L)
5= moves LE (R or L)

6=oral motor movement
7=vocalizes
8=visually tracks
9=change in facial expressions
10=other response (specify)
+=correct response to commands

Developed and used with permission by Ann P. Gervin, MT-BC

Figure 2. Music Therapy Coma Stimulation

- Therapists and family members should refrain from talking and laughing loudly while in the room.
- There should be minimal noise from the hall. Close the patient's door to mute background noise.

To the Music Therapist: Working With the Patient

As with any patient, introduce yourself each time you work with the patient. Concisely explain in simple terms what you are doing and what you want him/her to do. Address the patient by name. For instance, "Hi John. My name is Liz. I'm the Music Therapist. I'm going to ask you to follow some directions. I want you to do them the best that you can."

Patients may hear what you are saying and have some understanding of it, so don't discuss unfavorable things about patients in front of them. Treat them with respect, just as you would with any other person. Just because patients' eyes are closed or they aren't moving, doesn't mean they can't hear or understand what you are saying.

Finally, there are two important concepts in working with all levels of brain injury patients: repetition and structure. Create your therapy sessions to incorporate these two concepts.

Treating Agitated Patients

Agitated patients can be extremely difficult and frustrating to deal with. Some patients cry; other patients verbally or physically abuse themselves or others. In general, they are responding to their own inner confusion and any external stimuli can easily set them off. If a patient is agitated, try to define triggers. Triggers might be certain auditory or visual stimuli, family members, or maybe they're simply tired.

To the Music Therapist: Working With Agitated Patients

Do not confront or antagonize these patients. If patients insist they are not in a hospital, for instance, simply correct them gently but firmly and move on: "I know you think you are in a train station, but this is really a hospital. I am Jeff, your music therapist." Then continue with another topic. By no means should you argue the point, as this will only escalate behavior.

If patients do become agitated, take them to the nearest area with the least amount of stimulation possible. Even dimming the lights may help. Speak slowly in a low, gentle, calming voice and use simple, concise language. Smile and reassure them that they are safe.

If patients are very agitated, it is very likely that you will not meet your set therapy goals during your time with them. In fact, their scores may decline. This is normal and does not make you a bad therapist. You will have to lower your expectations regarding goals until they work through this agitation. Realizing this will make therapy sessions less frustrating for you because you won't feel so pressured to reach stated goals during therapy.

Behavior modification therapy may not be an appropriate option for the severely agitated patients in a rehabilitation setting for a variety of reasons. First of all, it is extremely difficult to maintain a consistent environment in a hospital due to the amount of staff involved in a patient's care. In most hospitals, nurses change shifts and rooms, and therapists have to cover other therapists' patients. Another reason behavior modification may not be appropriate is that many professionals feel agitated patients cannot reason at this stage. Therefore, they probably do not have the cognitive ability to realize whether they are being rewarded or punished for a particular behavior, especially at the beginning of the phase.

Therapy with an agitated patient can be frustrating and confusing for therapists. Some professionals believe that patients should be able to stay in their rooms and have minimal therapy (if any at all) to decrease stimulation and thus hopefully decrease agitation until the phase passes. However, many insurance companies insist each patient must have a specified number of hours of therapy each day for reimbursement. Therefore, patients sitting in their rooms receiving little or no therapy is not a practical solution.

Other professionals believe that repetition and structure are so important with these patients that a regular therapy schedule should be maintained as much as possible. They believe it is important for therapists to be as firm as possible and to require the patient to sit in the therapist's office for the entire scheduled time doing nothing, if necessary, to maintain structure and discipline. These therapists may tell patients they have to sit there until a certain time, and they can monitor the clock if they desire.

Again, every patient is different and it may be necessary to experiment with different tactics to get the best results with each person. In addition, therapists develop their own strategies and ideas to treat agitated patients. As mentioned above, opinions vary among professionals. Learn the policies and methods of your hospital for dealing with such patients. It may be a good idea to have the team of therapists get together and develop a uniform way of dealing with agitated patients to ensure the therapy process remains structured, consistent, and effective.

Goals for Patients With Traumatic Brain Injuries

Appropriate goals for any type of therapy depend upon the patient's level of functioning. Table 1 displays a general guide to appropriate goals for traumatic brain injury patients in relation to the Ranchos Los Amigos Scale and may be used as a starting point for selecting activities appropriate to the different levels. Initial goals and activities focus primarily on basic functional skills. As awareness, orientation, and function increase, the therapeutic emphasis gradually shifts to psychosocial function and emotional coping.

Table 1

Music Therapy Opportunities Corresponding to the Ranchos Los Amigos Scale

Ranchos Los Amigos Scale Level	Music Therapy Opportunities
Ranchos Level I: *No Response* · Patient is completely unresponsive to any stimuli	· Therapist presents stimulating and sedative music selections while monitoring pulse fluctuations, physical movements, and/or vocalizations
Ranchos Level II: *Generalized Response* · Reacts inconsistently and nonpurposefully to stimuli in a nonspecific manner · Responses may be physiological, gross body movements, and/or vocalizations	· Responds physiologically to music selections · Visually tracks instrument · Plucks guitar strings on commands · Localizes sounds
Ranchos Level III: *Localized Response* · Reacts specifically but inconsistently to stimuli · May respond to simple commands inconsistently · May exhibit delayed responses · Respond require augmentative communication (i.e., pictures)	· Localizes sounds · Visually tracks instruments · Plucks guitar strings on command · Follows simple commands · Supplies vocal automatic responses to very familiar songs · Imitates drumming patterns
Ranchos Level IV: *Confused, Agitated* · Severely decreased ability to process information · Responds primarily to his/her own confusion · Behavior is frequently bizarre and nonpurposeful · Verbalizations are often incoherent	· Listens to familiar music · Exhibits relaxation response · Imitates drumming patterns · Follows simple commands · Performs song lyric completions
Ranchos Level V: *Confused, Inappropriate, Nonagitated* · Alert and able to respond to simple commands fairly consistently · Highly distractible; lacks ability to attend to task · Verbalizations are often inappropriate · Complex commands responses are nonpurposeful, random	· Attends to task · Follows written schedule or picture cues · Follows commands, simple and complex · Performs simple writing, sequencing, and auditory sequencing tasks · Utilizes mnemonic devices

Ranchos Los Amigos Scale Level	Music Therapy Opportunities
Ranchos Level VI: *Confused, Appropriate* · Goal-directed behavior · Follows simple directions consistently and shows carry-over · Past memories show more detail than recent memories	· Contributes to writing of rehabilitation goal song · Performs more complex auditory sequencing · Performs lyric analysis · Completes symbol substitution worksheets · Contributes to simple song writing
Ranchos Level VII: *Automatic, Appropriate* · Appropriate and oriented within hospital · Goes through daily routine automatically · Has shallow recall of recent events · Lacks insight into judgment and problem-solving deficiencies	· Revises rehabilitation goal song as appropriate · Contributes to song writing · Performs multi-task activities · Performs complex auditory sequencing · Performs lyric analysis
Ranchos Level VIII: *Purposeful, Appropriate* *(standby assistance)* · Consistently oriented to person, place, and time · Sustains attention and task completion with distraction · Uses assistive memory devices · Is aware of culture, past, and present events · Independently learns new tasks · Demonstrates increased abstract reasoning and tolerance for stress · May be self-centered, argumentative, depressed · Unable to recognize inappropriate social interaction or to anticipate problems	· Revises goal song as appropriate · Engages in active listening for social communication · Engages in turn-taking activities · Performs complex lyric analysis and songwriting addressing changes abilities · Identifies emotional supports and resources for coping · Identifies compensatory strategies
Ranchos Level IX: *Purposeful, Appropriate (standby assistance on request)* · Shifts between tasks · Uses assistive memory devices to recall daily schedule · Identifies consequences of actions · May experience continued depression, irritability, and low frustration tolerance · Self monitors appropriateness of social interaction · Acknowledges impairments and problem-solves	· Utilizes logbook, schedule or planner · Revises goal song as appropriate · Performs complex lyric analysis and songwriting addressing psychosocial issues · Identifies emotional supports and resources for coping · Identifies adaptive meaningful leisure and community activities · Initiates use of compensatory strategies
Ranchos Level X: *Purposeful, Appropriate* *(modified independent)* · Handles multiple tasks simultaneously with periodic breaks · Accurately estimates abilities and independently adjusts to task demands · Consistently engages in appropriate social behavior · Initiates use of memory and compensatory strategies · Recognizes needs and feelings of others · Periodically depressed, irritable, or exhibiting minimal frustration · Tolerant, particularly during periods of emotional stress	· Creates and maintains logbook, schedule, or planner · Develops realistic long-term goals · Initiates emotional coping activities, seeks out resources · Initiates adaptive meaningful leisure activities · Engages appropriately in community activities

Descriptions of Music Therapy Opportunities (Table 1)

Music and sensory stimulation: This is explained in the above section (coma stimulation).

Visually track instruments: Present an instrument (preferably bright colored). Have the patient follow with their eyes to the left, right, up and down. Observe the patient's ability to track in each direction. Do not play the instrument if you are only monitoring visual tracking or you will be giving auditory and visual cues.

Pluck guitar strings on command: Place a guitar or ukulele within grasping range of the patient. Place the patient's hand on the instrument if necessary. Tell him/her to "pluck the strings." This can carry over to "hit the drum," or something appropriate to the selected instrument.

Localize sounds: Play bells, drum, or another loud instrument out of the sight of the patient. Watch to see if patient turns to look for the sound.

Follow simple commands: e.g., "Hit the drum." Refer to pages 38-39 for a listing of commands.

Vocal automatic response/Song lyric completions: e.g., "Happy birthday to ___" . The goal is to elicit language through an automatic response. Refer to pages 34-35 for a listing of song lyric completions.

Imitate drumming patterns: e.g., "Frank, I am going to hit the drum. I want you to hit the drum the same number of times I do." Hit the drum one time, let him hit the drum one time. Use cues such as counting your hits and his hits if necessary. Then use physical assist with exaggerated movements.

Listen to familiar music: The goal is to attempt to decrease agitation.

Relaxation: The goal is to attempt to decrease agitation.

Simple writing tasks: Task levels vary according to language and attention capabilities; aphasia or apraxia may be present.

Simple auditory/visual sequencing tasks: - Includes both auditory and visual sequencing. For auditory sequencing, you play instruments while the patient has his/her eyes closed. He/She must tell you which instruments you played in the properly sequenced order. Visual sequencing involves placing instruments on a table while the patient is watching. Then have the patient close his/her eyes and tell you which instruments are on the table and in what order you put them there. Also, visual sequencing could include keeping a list, storyboard, or other visual aid of the session's activities and referring to it throughout the session. Refer to the chapter on cognition in this book for a more detailed explanation of sequencing.

Mnemonic devices: The therapist writes songs pertaining to daily activities, orientation, and/or names of family members to help the patient with memory and sequencing deficits. A goal song is an example of a mnemonic device and a song writing task, because each verse describes a primary goal from each therapy. For example, the first verse may be describing a goal from MT, and the second may be about OT. This can be a powerful mnemonic device.

Lyric analysis: Answering questions about song lyrics in order to improve reading comprehension, processing, insight, and writing skills. Written worksheets are given in the worksheet section of this book (pages 106-107).

Symbol substitution: Substituting one symbol for another requires higher level thinking and processing, sequencing tasks, and attention to task. Worksheets are given in the worksheet section of this book (pages 108-109).

Song writing/Goal song: Song writing, whether it is about hospital experiences or a favorite pet, can be very beneficial on many levels. In additional to the psychological benefits, the patient has to recall information and express it. Of course, this is especially challenging to anyone with language deficits. Another type of song is a goal song, where the song pertains to the patient's goals in each therapy. *See mnemonic devices above for more about goal songs.* The content of songs for those in higher stages of recovery may address changes in abilities, relationships with others, resources for coping, and long-term goal setting.

Multi-task activities: These are activities that require doing more than one thing at a time. For instance, playing the autoharp requires strumming, playing chords, attention to task, and reading music. Playing the keyboard requires visually tracking music, attending to task, color matching, and fine motor coordination. See the chapter on cognition in this book for a more detailed explanation and appropriate activities.

Complex auditory sequencing involves simple auditory sequencing of a given number of sounds, but playing each sample for a longer period of time, or requiring the patient to wait five or ten seconds before answering. This requires better memory and attention skills.

Active listening for social communication: Activities designed to increase attention to appropriate social interaction. Level of difficulty may progress from simple imitation of rhythms or lyric phrases to paraphrasing chosen lyric selections or self expressions.

Turn-taking: Vocal, instrumental, and movement activities that require reciprocal involvement or back and forth participation. Initial tasks, such as mirroring or "passing a rhythm" around the circle, provide more structure. Later tasks would require more independence and initiation, such as free improvisational call and response.

CHAPTER 3

✦✦✦

WEANABLE VENTILATOR PATIENTS

General Information

A ventilator is a machine that assists in the breathing process. It is attached to the outside of the tracheostomy tube, or trach, using a sort of hose-looking device. This hose is attached to the ventilator machine. There are several types of ventilators, each having some different features and settings. However, the modes of ventilation are relatively standard.

Control Mode means the ventilator is completely responsible for the patient's breathing, including the number of breaths per minute and the volume of gas the patient receives. Breathing exercises with a person on control mode would be futile because the patient can not breath on his/her own.

Assist Mode means the patient breathes as many breaths per minute as necessary, but the ventilator delivers a set volume of gas.

Assist Control is the same as assist mode, but if the patient does not initiate breaths, the ventilator resumes control mode.

SIMV, or Synchronized Intermittent Mandatory Ventilation, means the patient is allowed to breathe at his/her own rate and volume, in between the ventilator's set rate and volume. In other words, the ventilator has a set breathe rate and volume, and the patient can breathe intermittently at his/her own rate and volume.

CPAP, or Continuous Positive Airway Pressure, means the patient breathes spontaneously at any rate and volume. The ventilator delivers oxygen and positive end expiratory pressure, or PEEP, which simply means there is a pressure maintained in the lungs at the end of an exhalation.

Hospitals have policies regarding weaning patients off of a ventilator. The criteria might include the mode of ventilation the patient currently requires, and his/her *vital capacity*, which refers to the amount of air a person can inhale and then exhale. Another criteria may be a measurement of the patient's *arterial blood gases*, or ABGs, which is obtained through a blood sample. Among other things, ABGs measure the patient's oxygen and carbon dioxide levels to determine if the patient is receiving and exchanging the proper levels of oxygen and carbon dioxide.

The Weaning Process

Working with ventilator patients can be intimidating to an inexperienced therapist because of the very nature of the machine. The machine assists humans to breathe, one of the basic necessities of life. Every little cough or wince may immediately make entry-level therapists uneasy and wonder if they should call for help. Only experience with these patients can ease these feelings. Vent patients will cough, wince, have sore throats, have thick secretions, and often have a lot of anxiety. Psychologically, being on a vent is difficult for patients because they might feel their life depends on a machine run by other humans. These patients are no longer in control of their life.

Depending upon hospital facilities and various situations, these patients may have different goals, and, of course, a therapist needs to cater to these goals. Some patients may come to the hospital for a short time because the family needs to be educated about the vent before taking their family member home. Other patients can be weaned off the vent. The exercises and activities in this book are geared toward such a patient.

When a patient begins the weaning process, the hospital staff will turn off the ventilator for an amount of time during the day. This time off the vent is increased in increments over a period of days or weeks. However, these patients may still require oxygen, in which case they will have a portable oxygen tank that hangs on their wheelchair.

Often the next step is a compensatory speaking device. Many hospitals use *speaking valves*. Because a trach allows air to pass below the vocal chords, most patients cannot vocalize without a speaking valve. Some speaking valves can connect to the vent, in which case these patients may receive a speaking valve earlier in the rehab process while they are still on the vent. Some speaking valves connect only to a trach. These are used while the patient is not currently hooked up to the vent. Depending upon the goals for this patient, either may be appropriate during therapy.

When the patient's breath support increases, the trach is "plugged." This means a button-like device is placed over the opening of the trachoestomy tube. This is the final step before the trach is taken out, because it requires the patient to breath around the trach tube in the windpipe in a normal fashion, but it also allows the respiratory therapists to easily deep suction secretions through the trachea site if necessary by unplugging the trach.

When the patient consistently tolerates the plugged trach and can cough up secretions without assistance, the trach is pulled. This leaves the patient with a visible hole, or *stoma*, where the trach was formerly located. As the patient talks, one can hear air coming out of the stoma. A patient's voicing may be slightly breathy or temporarily decreased in volume because air is coming out of the stoma instead of traveling through the vocal cords. The medical staff will place a bandage over the stoma and the stoma will heal. To create a stronger, louder voice during this process, place your gloved fingers on top of the bandage and press lightly to assist in temporarily creating a tighter seal on the stoma. As the stoma closes, voicing usually improves.

More About Tracheostomy

To better serve the patients, a therapist should have a good working knowledge of vents and trachs. Although much of this information may be the responsibility of the respiratory therapists or even the speech therapists, it is important to be competent and understand the equipment involved. This section provides some basic definitions and descriptions of the mechanisms.

There are two methods of facilitating respiration: a *tracheostomy* and an *endotracheostomy*. An endotracheostomy is a trach that goes into the patient's mouth and down the windpipe, or *trachea*. This is used if mechanical ventilation is necessary for a short period of time, i.e., a few days. This chapter is geared towards patients with a trachoestomy, which is a tube placed in the windpipe through an incision in the neck. A tracheostomy tube, or trach, is placed in the hole, or stoma, to facilitate breathing.

There are many different types of trachs. They may be made from a variety of materials, including PVC and silicone. Trachs come in different sizes and varying degrees of flexibility. They may or may not have an *inner cannula*. Some trachs have a *cuff* and some do not.

The material a trach is comprised of can affect a patient in a few ways. For instance, PVC is stiff. Because everyone is a little different, the tube may feel uncomfortable or even irritate a person's trachea. PVC is also a pourous plastic, and bacteria or extra tissue can grow on the material. However, PVC is disposable and economical. Silicone, on the other hand, is flexible, which may prove to be more comfortable for a patient. Silicone is a less permeable material, resulting in less potential for bacterial or tissue growth on the apparatus. However, it may be more expensive (Kazandjian & Dikeman, 1998).

The main tubing section is called an *outer cannula*. An *inner cannula* is a tube placed inside the outer cannula that can be removed when necessary. It is important that the outer cannula has a large enough opening if an inner cannula is to be used, or the actual opening available for air may be decreased tremendously. For this reason, inner cannulas are usually used only with adult trachs.

Inner cannulas are useful in particular situations. Sometimes a patient may have a mucous "plug," or a large mucous obstruction, in the inner cannula. Respiratory therapists can easily and quickly remove the inner cannula and replace it with a new one if necessary.

A *cuff* is a balloon-like feature of a trach that creates a seal between the trach tube and the trachea (see Figure 3). A cuff can be inflated or deflated using a syringe full of air or saline. When the cuff is inflated, the balloon-like feature fills the windpipe so that secretions, saliva, or blood can't fall down the trachea and into the lungs. However, the cuff is not designed to stop food or liquid from falling down the trachea.

Unfortunately, many professionals do not realize the importance of not over-inflating the cuff in the patient's trachea. An over-inflated cuff can cause irritation as well as cause the tracheal walls to stretch and actually decrease the size of the epiglottis, which in turn can affect swallowing abilities.

When a cuff is deflated, it allows air into the upper airway. *It is crucial to deflate the cuff before placing a speaking valve on a patient to avoid suffocating the patient.*

Speaking Valves

This is a device that fits over the trachea site so that the patient may talk more effectively. Placing a speaking valve on a patient is not difficult, but hospitals and therapists may have policies in place stating only certain professionals may place the valve on a patient. They may also have policies regarding suctioning mucous externally around the trach site, filling oxygen tanks, and changing patients from the wall oxygen unit to a portable tank so they may leave the room. Learn your hospital's policies.

There are a variety of styles and features of speaking valves, and there are many types of speaking valves. Some speaking valves attach to the vent, and some are used after a person is weaned off the vent. They are placed directly on the trach, but the details vary slightly from speaking valve to speaking valve. However, usually air enters through the speaking valve and is exhaled through the mouth. Patients often report being able to obtain some air through their nose while inhaling as well. Learn how the speaking valves in your facility operate so you utilize the appropriate breathing exercises. Depending on the type and style, it may be possible to connect oxygen to the speaking valve so the patient still receives the necessary amounts of oxygen. Humidification can fit over the valve so the oxygen is not too dry.

Stronger patients may be able to get voicing around the trach without using a speaking valve. This is called *leak speech.* Although leak speech does not hurt or strain the vocal cords of the patient, it is a difficult task to accomplish. Most patients require a speaking valve to get voicing.

The speaking valves available on the market now are much easier to place and much easier to tolerate than some products in the past. It is important to note that when using certain speaking valves, a patient may cough when it is first placed over the trach opening. This is natural and is no cause for alarm. The air being redirected through the throat,

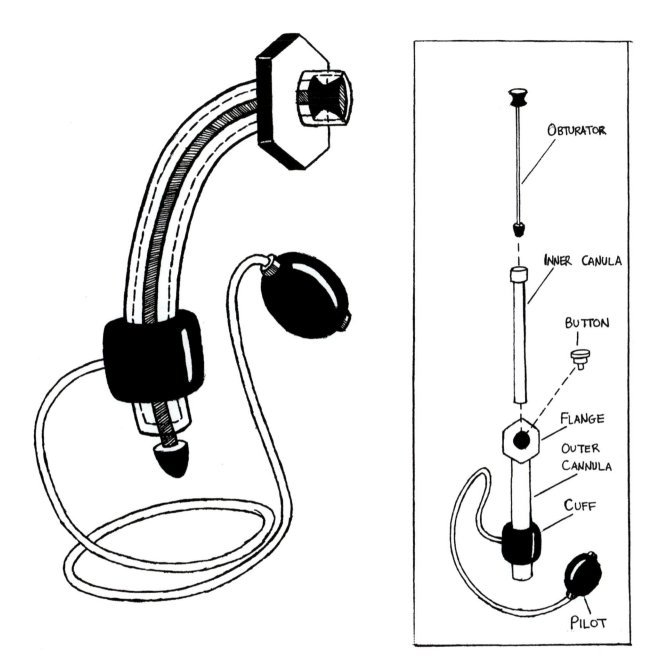

Figure 3. Labeled Drawing of a Tracheostomy Tube with a Cuff

nose, and mouth often tickles or is simply a drastic change that makes many patients cough.

Although the patient usually informs you when they cannot tolerate the speaking valve any longer, the decision sometimes must be up to you. Some patients could be too scared or lazy to try and work through the initial coughing; some could be too congested and require deep suctioning by a respiratory therapist or nurse; others might try too hard to the point of slightly over-doing it. You must use your best judgment as to how much coughing is too much. Knowing and understanding each patient is the key. Having a respiratory therapist or an experienced person with you the first few times you work with a ventilator or trach patient is a good idea. If a patient has been very sick, check the chart, ask the respiratory therapist, or ask a nurse each morning to see what has occurred the night before.

To the Music Therapist: Monitoring Respiratory Patients

When administering therapy it is important to understand and monitor oxygen levels, heart rate, and other physiological changes if possible. There are portable machines available that measure heart rate, oxygen levels, as well as other parameters in a *nonintrusive* way that allows you to monitor these rates without drawing blood. Measuring ABGs, on the other hand, requires drawing blood, which is *intrusive*. While measuring ABGs is a good monitoring tool to assess the patient's ability to tolerate the use of speaking valves initially, this is not a practical resource during a daily therapy session.

The importance of understanding the above discussion can be demonstrated in this scenario. Your patient has a trach and a speaking valve. She is connected to a pulse oximeter, which displays the pulse, during therapy. She is also connected to a machine that measures oxygen saturation in the blood. Gradually you notice the patient's pulse is increasing, and oxygen saturation levels are decreasing. The patient seems to have labored breathing. She's becoming anxious, and begins to sweat.

These signs display some level of distress. Perhaps the speaking valve should come off. Perhaps you should notify a respiratory therapist or nurse. Understanding the equipment and the physiological effects of a person can be a vital element during therapy, not to mention knowing the hospital's policies and procedures in such a situation. Do you call respiratory or nursing? How do you reach them?

Goals for Weanable Ventilator Patients

Appropriate goals for weanable ventilator patients include but are not limited to:

- Increase breath support
- Increase tolerance of speaking valve (use time as a measurement tool)
- Increase vocal range
- Improve vocal quality
- Increase laryngeal elevation
- Increase oral motor strength
- Increase self-expression for adjustment and coping
- Increase locus of control through augmentative communication devices

The first two goals listed pertaining to increasing breath support require the breathing exercises located in Chapter 7 regarding respiratory exercises. Activities and techniques pertaining to the other goals listed above are discussed in Chapter 6 regarding dysarthria.

CHAPTER 4

✦✦✦

APHASIA

General Information

Simply put, aphasia is the result of damage to the part of the brain that controls language. Wernicke's and Broca's are areas of the brain that are responsible for language and communication. For most of the population, these language areas of brain are in the left hemisphere, regardless of right- or left-hand dominance. Therefore, stroke and brain injury patients who have left-brain damage and right-sided weakness or paralysis are usually candidates for aphasia. There are three basic types of aphasia: *expressive, receptive,* and *global.*

Types and Characteristics of Aphasia

Expressive Aphasia

People with expressive aphasia cannot say what they want to say, or they cannot "express" themselves. They often know exactly what they want to say, but they cannot think of the correct words. Some simply use the wrong word in a sentence; others cannot think of any words. They have great difficulty naming objects. These patients have word-finding deficits, an attribute referred to as *anomia.* They may *circumlocute,* or use phrases, descriptions, and/or hand gestures to explain an object without naming it.

Patients presenting expressive aphasia may not be able to write anymore because they cannot remember how to write letters, come up with the correct word, and/or sequence to the letters to spell words. In addition, they may have to learn to write with their left hand due to their right-hand weakness or paralysis, which further exacerbates this frustrating situation.

Receptive Aphasia

A person with receptive aphasia has lost the ability to understand information or language. When someone talks to a receptively aphasic patient, it may seem like a completely different language to that patient. Consequently, these patients may have reading deficits as well.

Global Aphasia

Patients with global aphasia are both severely receptively and expressively aphasic. These patients often do not respond to verbal instructions, or they respond with an automatic word, phrase, or gesture.

Scholars and aphasiologists use different terms to describe aphasias in an attempt to have more specific descriptions of the characteristics of aphasia. Speech pathologists and other professionals will use these terms, so it is important to have a basic knowledge of the most commonly used terms. These are some of the more common descriptions of aphasia.

Aphasias can also be described as *fluent and nonfluent.*

Fluent aphasia refers to speech that is fluent but contains word or sound substitutions, or simply unintelligible words. The words flow easily, although they may be incorrect or inappropriate in the context. There are three basic types of *fluent aphasias*: conduction aphasia, transcortical sensory aphasia, and Wernicke's aphasia. Of the three, Wernicke's aphasia seems to be the term most frequently used in the therapy setting.

Wernicke's area of the brain, named after 19th century German physician Carl Wernicke, is responsible for processing language. The primary characteristic of Wernicke's aphasia is impaired auditory comprehension but very articulate (although slightly impaired) speech. Patients with Wernicke's aphasia may be able to conduct "small talk" with family and friends, but their naming skills may be severely impaired. They may not correctly understand the word you just told them; thus, they may not be able to repeat it back to you (Chapey, 1994). Often professionals simply refer to this presentation as receptive aphasia.

Nonfluent aphasia is simply *jargon*, or unintelligible utterances. Production of each word is labored. There are three types of *nonfluent aphasia*: Broca's aphasia, global aphasia (see above), and transcortical motor aphasia (Chapey, 1994). Of these three, global and Broca's aphasia seem to be the terms most commonly used in the therapy setting.

Broca's area in the brain, named after a 19th century French physician, is responsible for producing speech. Broca's Aphasia, therefore, characteristically exhibits a small vocabulary, uncoordinated articulation (apraxia), and only the most overlearned words and phrases. However, auditory comprehension is relatively good. Writing and speech are impaired, but reading displays only mild deficits (Chapey, 1994). Professionals often refer to this presentation as expressive aphasia.

As with anything else, each person is different and therefore each person's aphasia is different. Generally patients have a mixture of expressive and receptive deficits. Some patients *perseverate*, or continually repeat a word or phrase again and again. Some patients tend to repeat what was just said to them, which is known as *echolalia*. Reading cues may facilitate communication between patient and therapist; other times they provide no help at all.

To the Music Therapist: Working With Aphasic Patients

Stay on your toes; some patients nod or say "yes" and "no" all day long, but they may not understand a word anyone is saying. Some patients stay perpetually (and understandably) frustrated, while other patients have a wonderful sense of humor and can laugh at the nonsensical jargon that pours out of their mouths.

Regardless of their attitude, it is very important to encourage and be sensitive to the needs of aphasia patients. During therapy, it is important to practice talking and building confidence. When trying to communicate with an aphasic person, speak *slowly*. For patients with severe deficits, ask simple yes/no questions ("Did you take your pills?"). Use simple words and phrases—remember, to the patient, you're practically speaking a foreign language! If the patient doesn't understand the first time, try to rephrase the question in simple terms.

Some aphasic patients may have an augmentative communication device, such as a picture board. If they do, use your own pictures to facilitate therapy, as well as give the patient practice using the device. Often the speech therapist will determine if this is appropriate for the patient. Many aphasics cannot use these devices, however, because it requires a certain amount of cognitive ability to recognize the picture, understand it is a symbol for an object or action, and understand the effect of pointing to that picture.

As with any other diagnosis, treat the patient age-appropriately. Patients with aphasia may not understand your words, but they *will* understand your facial expressions, body language, and tone of voice. If patients suddenly appear anxious and they are trying to tell you something, one of the therapist's first guesses should be, "Do you have to go to the bathroom?" After this important question is resolved, take the time necessary to figure out what the patient does want. A drink? Some food? "Talk with your hands" if necessary to facilitate communication.

Goals for Patients With Aphasia

Appropriate goals for patients with aphasia include but are not limited to:

- Increase automatic responses
- Increase object identification
- Increase the ability to recognize object function/describing an object

- Increase following directions
- Increase the ability to match objects, colors
- Increase body part identification
- Increase writing skills
- Increase reading skills
- Increase imitation
- Increase auditory sequencing ability
- Increase communication of basic feelings and preferences

Appropriate Activities and Important Concepts

Automatic Responses /Song Lyric Completions

Finish this song phrase in your mind, "Happy birthday to _____."

Did you automatically think "you"? That is an automatic response. Many aphasic people have the ability to say words automatically in phrases, songs, during conversation ("yep") or simply when they feel emphatically about something (i.e., swearing when in pain or frustrated, saying "no," "ouch," or "Lord, have mercy" when it is almost like a knee-jerk reaction). In general, automatic responses are responses that come naturally (or automatically) and do not require thought. Music facilitates automatic responses because music is processed in different areas of the brain from language and can allow the patient to respond without relying on the affected language areas. In addition, the words are already set in the song (no need to conjure words to form a sentence) and the melody and rhythm facilitate the whole process. Speech therapists use proverbs, clichés, and "opposites" (i.e., up/down, black/white, etc.) and other automatic responses to facilitate speech. Incorporating these into songs can be challenging but fun for music therapists and patients alike.

Therapist's Directions: Sing the beginning of the phrase, then gesture to the patient to fill in the blank. For a higher level patient, instruct the patient to sing the whole phrase and/or song immediately after he/she has filled in the blank. Of course, it is necessary to use songs that your patients knew premorbidly. If a person does not recognize a song, try a different song and do not penalize their percentage while taking data.

Spoken directions: I am going to sing part of a song and I want you to finish it.

1. Happy birthday to _____.
2. Twinkle, twinkle, little _____.
3. Deck the halls with boughs of holly, fa la la la la, la la la _____.
4. Down in the valley, valley so _____.
5. Gonna lay down my burden, down by the river _____.

6. Bicycle built for _____.
7. Jingle bells, jingle bells, jingle all the _____
8. Oh I come from Alabama with a banjo on my _____.
9. I've been working on the rail _____.
10. Rockabye baby, in the tree_____.

More Song Lyric Completions

1. Twinkle, twinkle little _____
2. ... look away, look away, look away, _____
3. Would you like to swing on a star, carry moon beams home in a_____.
4. Oh give me a home, where the buffalo _____.
5. When Irish eyes are _____.
6. London bridge is falling _____
7. You ain't nothing but a hound _____.
8. Baa baa black sheep, have you any wool? Yes, sir, yes, sir three bags _____.
9. I'm looking over a four-leaf _____.
10. Somewhere over the _____.
11. Shine on, shine on harvest _____.
12. Let me call you sweetheart, I'm in love with _____.
13. For he's a jolly good _____.
14. Oh when the saints, go marching _____.
15. ... down came the rain and washed the spider _____.
16. Old MacDonald had a farm, E I E I _____.
17. Oh my darlin', oh my darlin', oh my darlin' _____.
18. Pardon me boys, is this the Chattanooga _____.
19. Jesus loves me this I know, for the Bible tells me _____.
20. ... tripped the light fantastic, on the sidewalks of New _____.
21. Take me out to the ball_____.
22. Don't step on my blue suede _____.
23. Michael row the boat ashore, Hallelu_____.
24. Amazing grace, how sweet the _____.
25. My country tis of thee, sweet land of _____.
26. Should auld acquaintance be _____.
27. Frosty the _____.
28. These are a few of my favorite_____.
29. Doe, a deer, a female _____.
30. My Bonnie lies over the ocean, my Bonnie lies over the _____.
31. Oh, bring back my Bonnie to _____.
32. Daisy, Daisy, give me your answer _____.

Object Identification

Identifying objects is an important exercise. Practice saying and naming instruments. If reading/writing is a goal, show index cards with the name of the instrument clearly printed. For higher level aphasics, ask them to describe the instruments and/or their function (the drum is *round*, you *hit* the drum, you *shake* the bells, you use them to make music, etc.) Making sentences using the word "drum" can be extremely challenging as well.

Using pictures to identify common instruments is helpful, although be careful not to become too technical. For instance, the average person in your community may not be able to identify a euphonium. Asking a stroke patient to do this task may be unreasonable. However, attempting to identify a piano or a guitar is very appropriate.

Basic concepts used in music translate into events in everyday life as well. For instance, up/down, slow/fast, loud/soft, start/stop are all basic concepts. They can be explained in a musical context quite easily.

Identifying body parts is important, too. "Head, Shoulders, Knees, and Toes" can be a valuable song because it is repetitive and popular. There are many wonderful children's songs that teach basic concepts such as body part identification and colors; however, take caution as to which ones you choose for adult patients. Sometimes a therapist is able to get around such inconveniences by lowering the key of the song or introducing it as, "This may be a song you sing with your grandchildren." However, recordings with children singing in the background are better left for children.

Object Description

Object description is a higher level task which involves not only naming the object but describing it: what it does, what it looks like, how it sounds, etc. Place an instrument on the table and ask the patient to describe the instrument. You may need to physically show the patient how it is played, then he can verbally tell you how to play it. As the patient improves, have them tell you three things about each instrument.

Melodic Intonation Therapy

Melodic Intonation Therapy is an amazing technique that really shows off the power of music. This technique seems to be most successful with patients who have relatively good comprehension skills. The general idea is to form simple words or phrases by singing them, using the natural inflection used in regular speech patterns. Use mainly 1 and 3 in a scale, so the melody doesn't become too complicated; basically it's either up, down, or the same note. As you sing the word, take the patient's hand and beat each syllable to the rhythm. Make sure patients are looking at your lips because it helps them imitate lip and tongue postures, etc. For example:

' \ ,   (3 to 1)

bath room

Repeat it again a few times. Then try to fade out the melody and ask the patients to say it plainly. Then ask, "What do you need?" to which they attempt, "bathroom."

Try to use practical phrases at first so as to empower the patient with basic needs. For instance, "hungry," "water," "thank you," "yes," "no," "help me," "call the nurse," "doctor," etc. While the patient won't be able to say these words spontaneously right away, it eventually can be a very powerful therapeutic tool. This exercise can also give hope to those who haven't heard themselves say an intelligible word in a couple of weeks.

Following Commands

This is a great task for object identification and comprehension. However, it is important to realize that the aphasic patient might be able to comprehend, but just not be able to identify which instrument is in question. If this is the case, begin with simple tasks like, "Which one is the drum?" or "Show me the drum." At this level, present only two instruments (also called a "field of two"). Introduce one instrument, then the other.

For higher level patients, introduce three instruments on a table (a great opportunity for naming objects). Then explain that you are going to ask them to follow some commands. If, for instance, you have a hand bell and a drum, say, "Hit the drum." Wait for them to complete the command. If patients do not, model it. Then if necessary, physically assist them to complete the task. Continue with "shake the bells," "touch your nose," and so on. Doing a set of 10 commands allows the therapist to take a quick percentage of successful responses and obtain objective, measurable data. For patients with severe receptive deficits, it is a good idea to use the same 10 commands each time. Remember to take note if the patient requires physical assistance, therapist modeling for imitation, or frequent repetition of the command. See the list of commands in the following pages.

Begin with a "field of three," or three instruments on a table placed in front of the patient. As the person advances, a field of four or even five may be used. Remember to introduce each instrument each therapy session, and have the patient repeat the name.

As the patient becomes consistently better at one step commands, add a set of two-step commands (shake the bells, then hit the drum), and eventually three-step commands (shake the bells, hit the drum, then touch your nose).

Simple One-Step Commands

Therapist's Directions: Say the command. If the patient does not respond appropriately, give verbal cues such as, "Which one of these is the drum?" and gesture toward the instruments. If the patient still does not respond, slowly assist the patient in doing the task.

Practice it one time afterward by saying, "Let's try that again—hit the drum" and immediately assist again if necessary.

Spoken directions: "I am going to give you some directions and I want you to follow them."

1. Hit the drum.
2. Shake the bells.
3. Touch your nose.
4. Shake the maraca.
5. Point to the door.
6. Hit the drum.
7. Shake the maraca.
8. Make a fist.
9. Shake the bells.
10. Smile.

Simple Two-Step Commands

Spoken directions: "I am going to give you some directions and I want you to follow them in the order that I tell you." (Note: If patients are having difficulty with two-step commands, it may benefit them to start with a "standard" second step. In other words, the second step may be "... and hit the drum" for each command.)

1. Hit the drum, then shake the bells.
2. Point to the ceiling, then point to the floor.
3. Tell me your name, then hit the drum.
4. Shake the maraca, the shake the bells.
5. Touch your nose, then shake the maraca.
6. Point to the door, then point to me.
7. Shake the maraca, then hit the drum.
8. Shake the bells, then shake the maraca.
9. Hit the drum, then smile.
10. Shake the bells, then hit the drum.

Complex Two-Step Commands

Complex commands involve using "before" or "after" in the command.

Spoken directions: " I am going to give you some directions and I want you to follow them in the order that I tell you."

1. Hit the drum after you shake the bells.
2. Shake the maraca before you hit the drum.
3. Touch your head before you open your mouth.

4. Point to the ceiling after you point to the floor.
5. Shake the bells after you make a fist.
6. Tell me if you are wearing earrings before you hit the drum.
7. Shake the maraca before you smile.
8. Tell me one thing you had for breakfast after you hit the drum.
9. Close your eyes before you raise your hand.
10. Shake the maraca after you shake the bells.

Simple Three-Step Commands

Spoken directions: " I am going to give you some directions and I want you to follow them in the order that I tell you."

1. Hit the drum, shake the bells, then touch your head.
2. Shake the maraca, hit the drum, shake the bells.
3. Point to the door, point to the floor, hit the drum.
4. Touch your nose, point to the ceiling, shake the bells.
5. Shake the bells, tell me your name, hit the drum.
6. Tell me one thing you had for breakfast, shake the maraca, point to your ear.
7. Open your mouth, hit the drum, point to the floor.
8. Shake the maraca, shake the bells, hit the drum.
9. Shake the bells, make a fist, tell me if you're wearing a dress.
10. Hit the drum, point to me, smile.

Complex Three-Step Commands

Spoken directions: " I am going to give you some directions and I want you to follow them in the order that I tell you."

1. Point to the door before you hit the drum and shake the bells.
2. Shake the maraca after you close your eyes and raise your hand.
3. Open your mouth before you shake the maraca and hit the drum.
4. Shake the bells after you point to your nose and point to the door.
5. Hit the drum after you shake the bells and point to your head.
6. Tell me one thing you had for breakfast before you shake the maraca and hit the drum.
7. Smile after you point to the ceiling and shake the bells.
8 Hit the drum before you point to the door and touch your knee.
9. Tell me your name before you shake the maraca and shake the bells.
10. Tell whether or not you're wearing a dress after you shake the bells and hit the drum.

Matching/Naming Colors

Playing color-coded bells, tone chimes, etc. is very appropriate for an aphasic patient, especially a person with receptive deficits. Use construction paper as an indicator of which instrument should be playing. For instance, a blue piece of paper might indicate the blue rhythm sticks or bells. In general, the therapy session seems to be most successful when the following steps are taken in sequence:

1. Introduce the instrument.
2. Introduce each color, asking the patient to name it and practice saying it correctly.
3. Explain the activity.
4. Practice holding sheets of paper and determining which instrument plays.
5. Do the activity (i.e., play the song).
6. Review the instrument's name and the colors used.

As an added level of difficulty, especially if this activity is used in a group setting with varying levels of deficits, encourage patients to play their instruments with their *affected* hand, using an adaptive device, if necessary. This adds a challenge to the person who has mastered the cognitive concept of matching.

Worksheets on pages 91 and 92 contain appropriate matching activities for this goal.

Singing

Singing any song can facilitate speech patterns and word formation. It is enjoyable to both therapist and client. It is also a great way to include an aphasic person in a group of nonaphasic people for socialization and self-esteem purposes.

Again, using familiar songs to elicit automatic responses is a key. If the patients didn't know a song premorbidly, it may be difficult for them to sing it now. Depending on your goals, popular songs with repetitive lyrics are usually a great choice. Try such songs as:

He's Got the Whole World	This Little Light of Mine
Down By the Riverside	Oh, Susanna
She'll Be Comin' 'Round the Mountain	I've Been Working on the Railroad
Row, Row, Row Your Boat	Take Me Out to the Ballgame
Shoo Fly	Jingle Bells
You Are My Sunshine	Amazing Grace
Down in the Valley	

As mentioned before, there are many wonderful children's songs that teach basic concepts and articulation sounds. While some of them can be used, some of them may need some introduction such as, "You may sing this with your children/grandchildren." Some should be avoided all together. Other good songs to use include:

Twinkle, Twinkle

Eensy Weensy Spider

Are You Sleeping?

ABC (often difficult; good for reading goals)

Old McDonald (naming animals and sounds)

When using such songs as "Old MacDonald" to name animals, it is much more effective if pictures of the animals are available to use as extra cues and teaching devices. When teaching language, words coupled with pictures or objects are the most effective.

Imitating Rhythms

Imitating drum beats or simple rhythms can be a challenging task to an aphasic patient if the area of the brain that processes auditory input has been damaged. Imitating rhythms requires attention and good listening skills, as well as the ability to imitate.

Ask the patient to hit the drum the same number of times that you hit the drum. Counting aloud may be necessary, as well as physically assisting the patient. Depending on their deficits, patients may display decreased initiation of tasks, or they might not understand the concept of imitation. By learning to imitate drum beats, patients will hopefully make the connection to imitate lip postures, gestures, and exercises needed in music and other therapies.

Writing Skills

Written worksheets provided in the back of this book (pages 85-115) are all appropriate for aphasic patients, depending upon their level. Not only are they trying to write with a language deficit, but their dominant writing hand may have been weakened, or left with no movement, causing them to write with their nondominant hand. Therefore, a tracing task is a good place to start. If your patient has difficulty seeing any letters, tracing over them with a thick black marker can help. Also, have some thick markers or pens available; some patients may require a bigger grip or thicker marker to hold.

Drawing music notes includes basic shapes used in drawing letters: circles and lines. These worksheets were placed in order of relative difficulty, so you must determine which, if any, are appropriate for your patients. Even though writing may not be a top priority goal, it can still be a worthwhile change in therapy, or a good task to do if you are called away on a meeting for a few minutes and your patients are able to work on their own.

Communication of Feelings and Preferences

Augmentative communication boards that display feeling words and pictures, song titles, pictures of instruments, and activity selections can be used to increase a patient's locus of control and interaction during the rehabilitation process. Communication of preferences and basic feelings facilitates increased emotional coping skills. Along with choosing activities, this board can facilitate song writing, orchestration of rhythm patterns, and other creative expression.

CHAPTER 5

✦✦✦

APRAXIA

General Information

Apraxia is defined by *Taber's Cyclopedic Medical Dictionary* (Venes, 1997) as the inability to perform purposeful movements although there is no sensory or motor impairment; the inability to use objects purposefully. When a person has apraxia, the correct message is sent from the brain to accomplish a task, but somewhere in the system the message is stopped or confused.

Types and Characteristics

Motor Apraxia

Motor apraxia refers to the difficulty of coordinating muscles in the body. For instance, patients with apraxia might not be able to point to their nose on command, but might actually point to different parts of their face, seemingly trying to "find" their nose. Typically patients' hands wander from their ears to their mouth, trying to find their nose. Apraxic patients might exhibit difficulty walking or completing daily living tasks like combing their hair, simply because they can't coordinate their muscles. Again, this is more of a coordination problem, not one of decreased strength or inability to comprehend the task at hand.

Oral Apraxia

Oral apraxia is exhibited by the difficulty or inability to coordinate movements of the lips, tongue, or vocal cords. Orally apraxic patients may not be able to stick out their tongue on command, or might even be *aphonic*, or unable to vocalize, simply because they can't coordinate the movement of the vocal cords with exhalation. Often this communication deficit is seen in conjunction with aphasia.

Verbal Apraxia

Verbal apraxia is the inability to form sounds or words due to lack of muscular coordination. Patients may know what they want to say, but the message gets mixed up when the brain relays the message to the facial muscles that would make the sounds. These patients may not be able to produce an "m" or "l" sound. Sometimes it is difficult to distinguish between aphasia and verbal apraxia.

Goal for Patients With Apraxia

An appropriate goal for patients with apraxia includes but is not limited to:

- Increase motor coordination

Accomplishing this goal requires patients to practice simple, controlled motor activities to regain control of their muscles, depending upon whether they have motor, oral, or verbal apraxia.

Appropriate Activities and Important Concepts

Upper Extremity Coordination for Motor Apraxia

Identifying and pointing to body parts is a great activity to increase upper extremity coordination and body part awareness. Using the "Head, Shoulders, Knees and Toes" song provides good musical structure and repetition for this activity.

Drumming is another effective way to promote hand-eye coordination. This requires a simple up-down movement that can be varied by changing the angle of the drum.

Picking up bells, shaking or ringing them, and putting them back on a table is another activity to promote control. Additional exercises include hand jives and clapping hands to the rhythm of some music. These are all simple tasks that require a certain amount of motor coordination.

Oral Postures and Placement

Some patients may be so completely apraxic that they cannot produce more than one sound. With these patients you will have to start from the very beginning. Vowel sounds are an appropriate place to start when practicing oral postures. Vowels are relatively easy sounds to make and they are necessary to form words. Practice the a, e, o, and u postures. Sustain each sound as if you were singing.

To produce "aaah," patients must open their mouths widely; "e" requires a smile; "o" requires them to round their mouths. To form a "u," patients have to pucker their lips. A person blowing through the recorder uses a "uuu" posture.

Practicing vowels and consonant-vowel sounds (such as "la") is very important for the severely apraxic patient. Singing such sounds as "la," "me," "go," "no," and any other consonant-vowel sound up and down the scale can be helpful in practicing oral postures, placement, and articulation. As the patients master one syllable, start to mix them: "la-le," or "me-la-go," which coordinates all the articulates.

If a patient responds favorably to automatic responses, then song lyric completions (page 34) can also help with placement. For instance, if patients have difficulty forming a "g" sound, which can be a difficult sound to imitate, try "Take me out to the ball_____." If they correctly produce the "g" sound, have them immediately reproduce it again. Then try to sing a word beginning with "g," such as "go," up and down the scale.

Relearning to stick out the tongue can take place with automatic responses as well. Try brushing a moist lollipop along patients' lips, then have them lick their lips. Lure patients' tongues by holding the lollipop tantalizingly in front of their mouth. Give a quick taste, then pull it away from the mouth again so they must stick out their tongue to reach it.

A therapist should be careful, however, when using this trick. Lollipops are loaded with sugar; avoid giving the patient too many "good" licks. It is always a good idea to check if the patient is diabetic or has any other food restrictions due to diet or upcoming medical tests.

In addition, lollipops stimulate the salivary glands, which could be an issue if patients are not to take anything by mouth ("NPO") and cannot handle their own secretions. Stimulating salivary glands means more saliva to swallow, which puts a severely dysarthric patient at risk for aspirating. Ask the speech therapists at your hospital for their opinions and preferences.

Aphonia

Aphonia is the inability to vocalize. There are several possible causes of aphonia, including paralyzed vocal cords and apraxia. Paralyzed vocal cords are usually diagnosed by a doctor, such as an ear, nose, and throat (ENT) doctor, and require different treatment than aphonia caused by apraxia. This section will deal with aphonia due to apraxia.

To the Music Therapist: Voicing and Breath Support

Some patients might be aphonic for a few days, while others may not be able to voice for weeks. Since voicing often automatically takes place while grunting, which can occur during physical exercise, coughing, clearing the throat, yawning, or laughing, a good strategy is to try to get patients to voice during one of these

---

instances. Try to make patients laugh, or listen for voicing during a yawn. Then have patients vocalize again immediately afterward so they can remember the feeling.

To vocalize, sufficient breath support must pass through the vocal cords to allow them to vibrate and produce sound. Quite often an apraxic patient may not be providing enough breath support. Some patients merely open their mouths but do not exhale at all through their mouths.

Recorders and harmonicas can be useful tools for providing immediate feedback when sufficient breath support has been expended. Keep in mind that the recorder requires less breath support than the harmonica. After patients have successfully blown through the instrument, immediately (but gently!) take it away from their lips and have them attempt an "aaaaaahhhhh."

It is important to remember that aphonia is extremely frustrating for the patient. While it should be a main focus of therapy, take a break if the patient shows signs of frustration. Switch gears and focus on some receptive or nonverbal tasks for a few minutes.

Continue to try a variety of tasks, because you never know when something might just "click" with a patient. Try to get patients to clear their voice ("a-hem"), which makes vocal chords come together, or push against your hand to grunt (like noisy weightlifters) in order to force the vocal chords together. Even blowing out a candle may enable the patient to exhale through the mouth automatically.

CHAPTER 6

✦✦✦

DYSARTHRIA

General Information

Dysarthria refers to the weakness often caused by a stroke that affects the oral, laryngeal, and/or respiratory muscles. Dysarthria affects the patients' ability to speak intelligibly, voice consistently, chew food, and clear the food from the mouth. Patients' tongues may be affected; therefore, they cannot enunciate words and may "pocket" food, or have chunks of food left in their cheeks. Patients might not be able to "handle their secretions" or drool. They might exhibit poor breath support, which will also affect their ability to cough and speak.

Types and Characteristics

There are several different types of dysarthria, but it is probably necessary to discuss only *flaccid* and *spastic* dysarthria.

Flaccid dysarthria refers to the muscles in the throat being flaccid, or weak. The facial muscles and/or respiratory muscles have decreased tone. Therefore, depending upon the severity of the weakness, the cheeks and lips tend to droop, especially on the affected side.

Spastic dysarthria means the patients' muscles become spastic and/or tight. Patients with spastic dysarthria in their throats often report feeling "strangled." Their voice may sound extremely forced and tense, and/or waver in and out.

Remember that dysarthria is primarily a muscular and motor issue, not a cognitive or receptive issue. Patients know what they want to say, and therefore the inability to communicate is extremely frustrating.

Goals for Patients With Dysarthria

Appropriate goals for patients with dysarthria include but are not limited to:

- Increase vocal range
- Increase vocal volume
- Increase oral motor capabilities by completing oral motor exercises
- Increase breath support
- Increase vocal quality
- Increase intelligibility
- Identify appropriate means of coping with frustration
- Develop short-term augmentative communication devices

Appropriate Activities and Important Concepts

Therapy for Flaccid Dysarthria

Oral Motor Exercises

"Mouth Aerobics": Select some popular music with a slow to moderate tempo to complete the following exercises. Repeat each exercise at least 10 times.

Have your patients shape their mouths to say "aaaah," then press their lips tightly together.

Next have them shape their lips to say "eeeee" (a big smile: let me see your teeth or gums!) then have the patients pucker their lips.

Have them stick out their tongues and move them from left to right in the corners of their mouths.

Tell your patients to put their tongue in their left cheek (on the inside of their mouth) and then the right cheek. Their cheeks provide resistance. Try to feel the tongue from the outside of their cheek. For added resistance, tell patients to press the tongue against your gloved finger or tongue depressor from the inside of their mouth.

Have your patients puff air in their cheeks like a monkey and hold it. For added difficulty, tell them to swish the air around in their mouth like mouthwash.

Next have them suck in their cheeks like a fish and hold it.

Experiment with other tongue movements to music, such as sweeping over the front of the teeth along the top, then along the bottom, as if you were clearing food. Tell them to try rubbing their tongue along the roof of their mouth from front to back as if they were removing peanut butter from the roof of their mouth.

Articulation: Sing "me," "la," "go," "key," "no," "bye," "moo," up and down a major scale. Use the keyboard to help cue yourself and patients. Then put different sounds together to practice coordinating the articulators.

For instance, try "me-la" on each note, "me-la-go," "harmonica," or even "buttercup." These words and consonant-vowel mixtures force your lips, tongue, and back of your mouth (the articulators) to coordinate and make sounds. For example, in saying "me-la-go," "me" requires lips, "la" requires tongue movement, and "go" requires the tongue in the back of the mouth.

When doing these articulation exercises, stress the importance of over-pronouncing these sounds and exaggerating mouth movements to produce these sounds. This is extremely important in improving patients' everyday speech, as well. If patients do not over-pronounce words, as well as speak slowly and loudly, they won't be understood as easily.

In the same respect, patients can practice over-pronouncing their words while singing songs, especially songs with good consonant sounds such as "K-K-Katy," and "My Bonnie."

Respiratory Exercises

Harmonica/Recorders: The harmonica and the recorder are great instruments for dysarthric patients because these instruments require good breath support and lip strength to play and produce sound. Dysarthric patients with decreased lip strength have a difficult time maintaining a proper seal on the harmonica or a recorder to create a note.

For more exercises regarding increasing breath support, see the Respiratory Exercises in Chapter 7.

Therapy for Spastic Dysarthria

In addition to sounding tense, the voices of these patients are quiet and inefficiently produce sound. The voice often exhibits an extremely inconsistent quality. These patients may also feel as though their throats "close up" during the day or night. While sustaining an "aaaahhh," a patient's voice may suddenly stop, or fluctuate in and out.

Relaxation

Relaxation exercises can be beneficial to a person with spastic dysarthria. Beginning a session with deep breathing ("breath in through your nose and out through your mouth") while listening to relaxing music may help to relax the throat muscles temporarily. There is a good chance the patient has been straining to make audible sounds all day, which in turn makes the muscles more tense.

Vocalization

Practicing a sustained "aaaahhh" with a relaxed tone is another good place to start. Using words that begin with a vowel sound or a soft "h" sound might facilitate voice production. Remember to have the patient take a nice, deep breath before saying the word or sound required for the task. This is most important, as many spastic dysarthric patients have poor breath support, which exacerbates the problem. These patients are not able to achieve sufficient breath support to speak loudly unless they first make the extra effort of taking a deep breath.

Song Lyrics

Utilize song lyric completions (pages 34–35) with songs that require the patient to say a word beginning with a vowel sound or a soft consonant, such as "He's Got the Whole World in His *Hands*." Practice these words using good vocal quality in a relaxed atmosphere. Remember to keep your voice low and calm, assuming the patient is not hard of hearing.

Singing

At times, singing can decrease some of the spasticity during therapy. You will want to experiment with a variety of methods. Sing a few Melodic Intonation Therapy phrases (pages 36–37) such as "How are you" to practice using these techniques with useful everyday phrases. As the patient's voice improves using the "soft" sounds (i.e., vowels, h's), graduate to consonant sounds that require an "attack," such as m, n, b, d, p, and eventually g, c, k.

Dysphagia

Possibly one of the most important issues for dysarthric patients is their ability to swallow safely. Dysarthric patients often have a weak swallow, allowing food to go down their windpipe. *Dysphagia* refers to a person's inability to swallow safely. If food or liquids enter the windpipe, dysarthric patients are often not strong enough to cough it up, and therefore they *aspirate*. Aspirating food or liquids can lead to pneumonia, or more specifically, *aspiration pneumonia*, because the food goes down the windpipe and into the lungs. Such an illness is a major setback to a stroke, ventilator, and/or brain-injured patient.

Simply put, the action of swallowing requires muscles to move the larynx (or voice box) superior and anterior in the throat. This process allows the epiglottis to cover the windpipe, and this, coupled with the vocal cords closing, prevents food from going down "the wrong way." This rise of the larynx is called laryngeal elevation.

After a stroke, the dysarthric patient's muscles are weakened and the larynx may not rise as high as it should. Therefore, the windpipe is not covered and the patient cannot complete a safe swallow. Patients sometimes report feeling "strangled" when they eat or drink thin liquids. For this and other reasons, speech therapists put patients on a diet that may consist of thickened liquids, pureed food, and mechanical soft ground meat. These special diet preparations increase the probability of a safe swallow.

To the Music Therapist: Vocal Exercises

Luckily, the muscles moving the larynx can be strengthened by doing laryngeal elevation exercises. So what are these laryngeal elevation exercises? Singing high pitches! Singing high pitches requires the larynx to rise in a manner similar to when the patient swallows. Therefore, vocal exercises that require singing low to high pitches, or any combination of the two, are extremely helpful to these patients. Sustaining a high pitch is sort of like isometrics for your swallowing muscles.

Goals for Patients With Dysphagia

Appropriate goals for patients with dysphagia include but are not limited to:

- Participate in and benefit from laryngeal elevation exercises
- Increase vocal quality and/or range

Appropriate Activities and Important Concepts

Laryngeal Elevation Exercises

The following exercises can be done in a group or individually.

Howling: Howling at the moon: "aaaaauuuuuuuuuuuuuuuuuuuu," requires a low "aaaa" and a high "uuuuuuuu."

Yodeling: "Yodel - ay - hee- huuuuuu"; start low on the "yodel-ay," hit a high pitch for "heee huuuuuuuu."

Sighing/Yawning: This is an old vocal warm up exercise from choir practice. Start in a high register and let your pitch fall down gradually, as if you are sighing or yawning.

Singing Intervals: Try singing octaves, 10ths, or any appropriate interval. Remember to target the highest pitch possible.

A keyboard can facilitate singing pitches because it gives patients an auditory cue or even goal for their voice to reach during the exercises. A keyboard can also objectively measure progress. Use your ear to determine what pitch a person is hitting. Then measure the increase in range through the therapy sessions. Is the vocal range increasing?

Mice: Have your patients make an extremely high pitch squeaking sound as if they are a small mouse. An "eeeeeek" sound as if they've seen a mouse can also be effective.

To the Music Therapist: Explain Yourself

Remember to educate your patients! Always explain why you are requesting that they do these exercises and the benefits involved. Most patients would not guess the benefits of yodeling and would find it absolutely ridiculous. Not only is it important to justify and explain what you are doing, but it is also important for you to educate the patients about their bodies and their deficits. Good, simple explanations of the exercises in conjunction with written lists and descriptions of exercises might motivate the patients to participate in these activities in their rooms and even after they are discharged from the hospital.

◆◆◆

MUSIC THERAPY AND RESPIRATORY EXERCISES

General Information

The following exercises and activities may be done individually or in a group setting. Since patients may not understand the concepts and benefits of these activities, you will need to review and discuss them frequently. The following topics should be included in your explanation:

1. Lungs expand and contract during normal breathing using the diaphragm, external intercostals, and the internal intercostals muscles, among others. These exercises help to strengthen these muscles.

2. Deep breathing can assist in "cleaning out your lungs" and "stirring things up a bit" (i.e., coughing mucous).

3. Good breath support facilitates daily physical activities.

4. Good breath support facilitates speech and provides sufficient volume.

5. Proper breathing techniques provide good breath support and relaxation.

6. Proper breathing techniques include:
   a. Having good posture.
   b. Breathing in through the nose and out through the mouth.
   c. Not raising the shoulders while inhaling; instead the stomach should inflate—much like a balloon.

Goals for Patients With Respiratory Needs

Appropriate goals for patients with respiratory needs include but are not limited to:

- Increase breath support for daily activities
- Increase vocal volume
- Sustain "aaah" for 15-20 seconds consistently

Appropriate Activities and Important Concepts

Slow, deep breaths with or without relaxing music can decrease anxiety as well as increase oxygen saturation in the blood. These exercises are appropriate for most patients with decreased breath support, including patients with chronic obstructive pulmonary disease, asthma, severe dysarthria, ventilator patients on certain modes, and persons with a tracheostomy. If patients are wearing a speaking valve, instruct them to breathe in through their nose and out through their mouths to the best of their ability. Air enters through the speaking valve; however, it is possible to inhale some amount of air through the nose. This is efficient breathing as well as relaxing.

Be sure to remind them to take a break if they start to get light-headed or dizzy. Passing out is not an objective! Also, reassure patients that they may begin to cough during these exercises. This is common and is usually because they are loosening secretions.

Exercises

The following exercises increase breath support and can be used with patients who have decreased breath support. With a little creativity, they can be completed as a group or individually.

Ho Ho Ho: "Give a big Santa Claus laugh from the belly." Actually, use the diaphragm. When this exercise is executed correctly, you should feel your stomach moving. Variations may include "Ho Ha Heeeee," varying length and pitch of last word (i.e., raising pitch from low to high to low again, etc.). Not only does this help to strengthen the diaphragm, but it also helps to get loud voicing. Classically trained singers and cheerleaders are taught to use their diaphragm to obtain volume without straining their voices.

This exercise may also be completed in the context of a song, such as "Up on the Housetop."

Reverse Breathing: Have patients exhale first, then inhale through their nose and out their mouth.

Holding Breath: Have patients inhale and hold for 5, 8, 10, 12, and 15 seconds, depending on the level of the patient for three or four trials. Try starting with 5 seconds, then 8 seconds the next trial, and so on.

Inhale Slowly/Exhale Slowly: Slowly inhale over a period of 5 seconds, then exhale normally. Do this a couple of times, then inhale normally and exhale slowly over a period of 5 seconds. Next, combine the two exercises by inhaling slowly over 5 seconds, then exhaling slowly for 5 seconds.

Sustaining AAH or OOOH: Taking in a deep breath through the nose, sustain a pitched "aaah" for as many seconds as possible. Many patients start with 2–3 seconds. Sustaining "aaah" for 20 seconds consistently is a good, challenging goal for adults. Variations on this exercise include sustaining "sssss," "mmmm," and blowing air with pursed lips.

Musical Instruments: Blowing into instruments such as harmonicas, recorders, kazoos, etc., require breath support and allow patients to practice holding pitches, playing songs, and following rhythmic patterns (echoing short, short, long, or quarter note, quarter note, half note).

Blowing on a certain word of a song is an easy activity for cognitively aware patients. For instance, "I'm going to sing 'Blow the Man Down,' and every time I sing the word *blow*, I want you to blow into your harmonica." As with any activity, it is usually a good idea to prepare the patients by stating that the word *blow* is always sung 3 times in a row during the song, i.e., *blow, blow, blow the man down.* Practice that section with the patients first. Then they are practically guaranteed success during the activity. Other possible songs include "This Little Light of Mine" (blow on *shine*), "Down in the Valley" (blow on *blow*), "B-I-N-G-O," (blow on each letter you would normally clap).

Blowing the instruments to recorded music can be fun, too. The "Blue Danube Waltz" lends itself to two short blows from each of two sections during the famous theme. If you have at least two patients in a group, divide them into two sections. Each section plays two notes. If this is an activity for one patient, that patient could play all four notes. The patients must pay attention to you during the entire section of music while you conduct so they know when to blow.

Teaching a B on a recorder and playing a song that requires many B's is another fun activity. (Alto recorders work well because of the spacing between holes for adult hands, and the more tolerable lower pitch—patients and innocent passers-by may thank you!) For instance, make cards that say "1," "2," "3," and "4." Play "Mary Had a Little Lamb," but every time a B should be played, hold up a card showing how many times the patients should blow their note.

As always, gear activities towards your patient's abilities or towards the group. For instance, playing the recorder requires a lot of attending, some fine motor skills, and following directions.

Blowing Bubbles: Blowing soap bubbles to music is a fun, relaxing, and creative way to practice breath support. As a variation, you can blow bubbles and the patients can try to keep them in the air by blowing. Remember to mention that this is a great activity for anyone who is returning home to a place with small children, grandchildren, cats, or dogs.

Children and some pets love to play with bubbles, and the patient can continue respiratory system exercise while playing with a child or pet.

Singing: Singing serves several purposes. It requires not only sufficient breath support, but also practice in breathing in the proper places in a song, i.e., between phrases. Singing also allows patients to practice good articulation, oral motor ability, and projection. With some patients, it might be appropriate to walk through the process of singing a phrase to a song, stopping and cueing to inhale, then singing the next phrase of the song.

Singing is also relaxing and fun. It is likely your patients do not have many opportunities to make choices during their day. Allow the patients to choose which songs they would like to sing. Provide songbooks to facilitate decision-making and participation.

Blowing Tissues, Paint, Paper Balls: Consider using a variety of other activities including blowing paper balls with straws, blowing paint with straws, or blowing crumpled tissues across the table. Sometimes these can be done in the form of a game, where two patients sitting across from each other must try to blow the object to their opponent's side.

Remember to keep in mind the cognitive levels of the group: low cognitive or apraxic patients may inhale through a straw instead of exhale. Therefore, blowing paint would not be appropriate.

To the Music Therapist: Share the Benefits of Music Therapy

Increasing breath support through music therapy exercises is a relaxing and beneficial aspect of the rehabilitation process, whether done individually or in a group. Frequently review the benefits of these exercises and activities with patients, and provide a written list and explanation of exercises so they can continue to benefit from them after they leave the hospital.

CHAPTER 8

✦✦✦

COGNITION

General Information

Cognition is an important issue when it comes to CVA, brain injury, and ventilator/trach patients. CVA and TBI patients in rehabilitation settings need cognitive training at some level. Of course, CVA and TBI patients both had insults to the brain, thus causing cognitive deficits. Ventilator patients may need cognitive therapy depending upon their recent medical history. For instance, the patient may have had an operation that caused anoxia, a stroke, or a car accident that resulted in respiratory failure.

Before implementing cognitive therapy with a patient, it is important to look at the medical and/or psychological history to rule out dementia. In later stages of dementia, cognitive training is unjustifiable because the person cannot remember or carry over any of the information given during therapy. Also, cognition is not reliably tested with patients with low levels of aphasia due to their inability to accurately relay information.

Goals for Patients With Cognitive Needs

Appropriate goals for patients with cognitive needs relate to, but are not limited to, the following issues in cognitive therapy:

Orientation: Being aware of person, place, situation (i.e., why they are in the hospital), date, and therapy session.

Memory: Short-term includes current session, or recall of session specifics; *long-term* refers to a task completed yesterday, or any information known for years.

Problem solving: The ability to propose certain solutions, anticipate their outcomes, and choose the best solution for the desired outcome.

Organization: The ability to group, arrange, sequence, or categorize concepts such as objects, ideas, and sounds.

Attending to task: The ability to pay attention or concentrate on the activity at hand.

Other Considerations

Impulsivity/Safety awareness: Impulsive patients will do things without thinking about them first, and, as a result, are great safety risks to themselves and others. If an instrument is placed in front of them, they will begin to play with it instantly and without any instructions. They may eat or drink too quickly and make themselves cough or choke. Worst of all, impulsive patients will often try to get out of their wheelchair, even if they cannot stand or walk.

Neglect: When patients have "neglect," it means they are neglecting or forgetting about their affected side. For instance, their head may be turned to the right, their eyes may even be shifted to the right, and they literally forget to look to their left side. Most likely these patients will eat food only on the right side of their plate and can't find their water unless it is placed in their field of vision.

Appropriate Activities and Important Concepts

A music therapy session can easily integrate activities for these cognitive areas with a little planning.

Orientation

Orientation is a great way to open a therapy session and, depending on the level of the patient, could be reviewed again at the end of a session. As usual, ask the patient an orientation question, give verbal cues, narrow down the choices to a field of two, then finally give the answer if necessary. Orientation can be done with a series of questions, a song, or both. An orientation song by itself might not require patients to come up with the answers themselves, but a "fill in the blank" song might present an opportunity to measure the progress of a patient. Orienting the patient, then using the answers to fill in the blank, provides some reinforcement and allows an opportunity to measure short-term memory abilities by immediately reviewing the facts. Using the song as a mnemonic device may also prove beneficial to the patient. As always, you must document correct and incorrect answers and take a percentage or an average. Look for trends, such as "patient has been oriented to person all week, but not to place."

When reporting orientation, some professionals report "patient orientated ×2" meaning the patient is oriented to two of the five orientation categories. Although it sounds professional, sometimes this type of notation can prove confusing. Other professionals might wonder *which two* is the patient oriented to: place and time, person and situation? Unless otherwise dictated by your facility, it might be better to specify the patient's exact orientation status.

Here are some common orientation questions:

1. What day of the week is it today?
2. What month is it?
3. What year is it?
4. What is this building/facility? (Is it a church, hospital, or store?)
5. Why are you in the hospital?
6. What therapy is this?
7. What is my name?

Memory

Memory is often a primary deficit for these patient populations. Short-term memory can be measured by asking questions at the end of the session regarding things that have occurred throughout that session. "What three songs did we sing?" "Which instruments did you play today?" and "What therapy did we say this was?" are all examples of questions to use. Ask 5 to 10 questions so that you are able to obtain sufficient data to calculate an accurate percentage for documentation. Keep in mind when taking data that remembering three songs should count as remembering three items! Information should be recorded on a data sheet like the one on page 85.

When working with severely impaired individuals, it might be necessary to say, "This is music therapy. What therapy is this?" and have them respond, "Music therapy." Surprisingly this can be a difficult task for some patients.

Long-term memory ability measurements could include such questions as, "What did we do yesterday?," "What did I want you to remember for today?" These should be documented for progress.

Problem Solving

In all honesty, problem solving can be the most difficult cognitive task to measure during music therapy. Speech therapy, therapeutic recreation, and occupational therapy have scenarios and vast amounts of materials available to them to test problem solving skills, such as, "What would you do if there was a fire in your home?"

Translating this strategy into music therapy requires some imagination. Depending upon the level of the patient, the word scramble worksheets provided in the worksheet section of this book (pages 110-112) might be an appropriate problem-solving task. Another activity is "Name That Tune," which requires deductive reasoning skills to determine the name of the tune. Play a few bars of familiar tunes on a keyboard and have the patients use their deductive reasoning skills to "Name That Tune." This can be accomplished individually or in a group. A list of possibilities include:

I've Been Working on the Railroad	Clementine
My Bonnie	When the Saints Go Marching In
Oh Susanna	Take Me Out to the Ballgame
Down in the Valley	Old MacDonald

Music therapists can also use situations that may occur during therapy, such as deliberately not plugging the keyboard into the electric outlet. "Oh, there is no sound when the patient presses the keys. Why not?" Well, maybe the keyboard is not plugged into the wall outlet or the power isn't turned on. Another great task is determining instruments for sound effects along with a story, poem, or song.

There are other situations during a session that also reveal patients' problem-solving skills, such as trying to maneuver their wheelchair out of your office at the end of a session. It is not unusual for patients to try to maneuver their wheelchair out the door, only to hit the same exact place in the wall over and over again. These patients simply back up, move forward, back up, and move forward repeatedly. They do not stop to think, to reason, to turn, or to ask for help.

Problem solving can also be addressed by the spelling practice worksheets on pages 100–102, song lyric analysis worksheets on pages 106–107, symbol substitutions on pages 108–109, the word scramble worksheets on pages 110–112, and convergent inferences on page 113.

Organization

Stroke and brain injury patients often have problems processing and expressing auditory and visual stimuli. While auditory and visual sequencing are organizational tasks that music therapists can easily work on, it is important to realize these tasks also require attention to task and short-term memory.

Place three instruments with very distinct sounds on a table in front of the patient. Introduce each instrument by playing it and identifying its name. Have the patient close his/her eyes. Practice first by playing only one sound so your patients can get used to the activity. This is called *auditory recognition*. When patients can name the instruments by their sounds, play two, three, or more sounds, depending upon the level of each patient. Then have the patients open their eyes and tell you which instruments were played in the correct order. This is called *simple auditory sequencing*. If patients have difficulty remembering the names of the instruments, have them point to the instrument and then name it to verify intentions. To add difficulty, have patients wait 5+ seconds before they answer you, or play the selections for a longer interval of time. This can be called *complex auditory sequencing*.

Visual sequencing can be practiced by placing the instruments on the table while the patients watch, then have patients tell you the order in which you placed the instruments. For added difficulty, you can cover the instruments with a towel and have them tell you which instruments are on the table.

Another visual sequencing task is a hand jive exercise. Do a sequence of motions, such as patting your knees, quietly snapping your fingers, then patting your head. Have the patient mimic you afterward.

Remember to take data! Do trials of 10 to obtain an easy percentage. If you are timing intervals, be consistent! Realize that the number of instruments used in the activity increases the complexity of the exercise. For instance, using only two instruments (field of two) in a session is a much easier test of abilities than using six instruments (a field of six).

Another organizational task requires *convergent* and *divergent* categorization. *Convergent* categorizing means you apply specific items to a group. For instance, you could ask your patients, "What do violins, guitars, and cellos all have in common?" They all have *strings*. *Divergent* naming requires the opposite: you give the category and they have to give the specific members. For instance, you could ask your patients to name three wind instruments.

Attending to Task

There are several different types of attention:

1. *Focused:* the ability to respond to stimuli
2. *Sustained:* the ability to pay attention over a period of time
3. *Selective:* attending while tuning out external distractions
4. *Alternating:* the ability to shift focus and attention between different tasks, for instance, doing paperwork, answering the phone, then continuing your work
5. *Divided:* attending to more than one thing at the same time, for instance, listening to the radio while driving a car.

Having patients attend to task is, of course, a vital goal. Any task demands attention in order to be completed. Playing instruments throughout the entire song, finishing a worksheet without cues for redirection to task, or doing a follow-the-leader activity all require attention to task. For documentation purposes, attention can be measured in seconds or minutes with or without frequent/occasional verbal cues for redirection.

Any activity requiring the patients to watch the conductor the entire song is an attention to task activity. Here are a few suggestions for activities that work well in group settings.

A therapist can utilize bells, handchimes, recorders, harmonicas, drums, and written worksheets. Bells and chimes are color-coded and handed out to patients. You hold up a colored piece of paper that matches the color of the bell or chime instrument when that note should be played in the song. Another method involves creating a poster or chart that substitutes colored circles for notes. Two great songs to color-code are "When the Saints Go Marching In" and "Love Me Tender." These songs require only five notes and they are both very popular songs.

Another alternative is to have the patients watch for your hand motions to know when to play or stop. Depending on your goals, you could create written signs with words such as "bells" or "drum" to let them know when to play. When you hold up the sign, the patients plays their instrument. When you put the sign down, the patients stop.

Still another attention exercise is "follow the leader" or a hand jive activity. This can be done individually or in a group. Play a popular song with a moderate tempo, preferably one without lyrics, so that the patients will not be as tempted to sing along and therefore become distracted. Instruct them to follow you. Perform hand jive motions to the rhythm of the music, such as patting the knees, clapping hands, or tapping your head. The patients must watch you during the entire song to know when to change motions. If this activity is done in an advanced group, everyone can have a turn leading one motion to the rhythm. Each patient can lead one motion, then point to the next person to lead the group with a motion, and so on.

Worksheets included in this book also serve as attention activities. Patients should be able to finish the worksheets without redirection from distractions. Depending upon the patient, some appropriate worksheets include lyric analysis (pages 106–107), copying notes (pages 93–95), and symbol substitutions (pages 108–109).

When attention to task increases, multi-task activities can be utilized. Multi-task activities are prevalent throughout a normal day of independent living. Cooking, watching television, and answering the telephone are all activities that are often completed simultaneously in an average day. People typically would be able to juggle their attention to perform all of these activities sufficiently.

People with decreased attention skills, however, might begin to heat a greased frying pan, become distracted by the television, and completely forget the hot frying pan. If they have to answer the door, they would forget about the television. By this time, the fire on the stove from the hot frying pan might become distracting to them!

Multi-task activities during music therapy include playing the keyboard and autoharp. For instance, playing a color-coded keyboard (while reading color-coded music) requires visual tracking of notes, attention, listening to tempo and/or other singers, hand-eye coordination, matching, fine motor dexterity, and possibly singing. Playing the color-coded autoharp (while reading music) requires visual tracking, listening to tempo and/or other singers, two upper extremity motions (strumming and pressing chords), gross and fine motor skills, attention, matching, and possibly singing.

Following Commands

Following one-, two-, and three-step commands are also appropriate exercises and goals for patients with cognitive deficits. These mental exercises require attention, short-term memory, and, in some cases, organization and sequencing skills. Lists of commands are provided in the chapter on aphasia in this book (pages 38-39). Worksheets addressing following written commands are on pages 103-105.

Neglect

Although neglect is caused by a sensory or perceptual deficit, it is included in this chapter because patients essentially require insight, memory, and attention to task in order to attend to their neglected side. As patients increase their insight and memory skills, they are usually more attentive to their neglected side.

Neglect refers to persons "forgetting" about the affected side of their body. For example, patients with a right-brain stroke may have left neglect. If you place instruments on a table to complete a simple commands task, the patients would have a hard time "remembering" or noticing the instruments placed on their affected side. Some patients have such severe neglect that their entire head is turned to one side and they look only at things on their unaffected side. Patients with severe neglect sometimes require physical assistance to turn their head to see in the affected direction, but will immediately turn it back when the physical assistance is removed.

Any activity requiring persons to attend to their neglected side is helpful. Sitting on patients' neglected side and placing instruments on a table on their neglected side requires the patient to attend to that side. An effective exercise involves having patients play every white key on the keyboard from their unaffected side to the affected side. Do the patients get to *midline*, or the center of their body? Do they cross midline? Monitor the amount of cueing and physical assistance this requires.

For another task, line bells or tone chimes along a table in a C Major scale with the low C on the unaffected side, and the high C on the affected side. Have the patient accompany you during "Do Re Mi," playing each note on your command. In this exercise, the patient plays "do" while you sing, "Doe, a deer, a female deer," and so on. It will be necessary to point to the correct bell or chime to cue the timing of the note as well as which bell or chime is next.

The drum is another useful instrument when working with neglect. Hold the drum at various angles and places in the area around the patient, especially on the affected side. With patients holding a mallet, have them reach for and hit the drum. If patients can't find it, hit the drum yourself to supply an auditory cue as to where the drum is located.

The worksheet pertaining to crossing out notes on page 90 in the back of this book also addresses neglect. The matching worksheets on pages 91 and 92 can also address neglect because the patient has to look to both sides of the paper and draw a line from one to the other.

If patients are having a difficult time looking at a particular item or person, place your hand in their view, instruct them to follow your hand, then slowly move it toward the item or direction in question. If this fails, take the patients' hand, instruct them to watch their hand, and slowly physically assist it over to the item.

If, after your therapy session, you must leave these patients to fend for themselves, ALWAYS place any water, or reminders, or important objects where they can find them. It is not fair to leave the nurses' call button where they cannot see it if there is nobody there to cue the patients to look to their neglected side. These patients will not look for things on their own accord and may attempt to do something unsafe because they cannot find what they need.

Impulsivity and Safety Awareness

The safety of patients is of paramount concern during recovery, the rehabilitation process, and after discharge. People who experience impairments leading to impulsive, unsafe behavior must be continually monitored. A variety of therapeutic activities, songs, or exercises are available to address this area of concern, for example, instructions such as, "I am going to put an instrument in front of you, but I don't want you to touch it until I tell you to." Slow drumming and deep breathing can be challenging for an impulsive patient. Writing a safety song can be a good mnemonic device, as well as writing the patients a note and placing it on their wheelchair where they can read it all day. These patients need constant supervision because they will try to do unsafe things without thinking twice.

The worksheets in the back of this book are another way to work on impulsivity. Often these patients will complete them so quickly that they make lots of errors. The worksheets pertaining to following written directions (pages 103–105) and word scrambles (pages 110–112) are appropriate to use. If they make a mistake on the worksheets, have them try to figure out where the mistake is. Remind them that is why they need to slow down and think before they do something.

Cognitive skills are a major issue for CVA , TBI, and some ventilator patients due to the nature of their injuries. As stated earlier, your primary goal is have the patient be as independent and self-sufficient as possible. For many of these patients, cognitive ability is a major factor in deciding their discharge plans and their future: whether they can go home by themselves, with a family member, or to a nursing home. Of course, patients' physical and financial status are also factors, but if they do not attend to task and have poor problem-solving skills, they must be supervised 24 hours a day. This kind of supervision may or may not be available in a patient's home.

CHAPTER 9

✦✦✦

UPPER EXTREMITIES

General Information

Many CVA patients admitted to a rehabilitation hospital have a weakened if not paralyzed affected side. This weakness will affect the whole right or left side of the body, depending on which hemisphere of the brain was damaged from t.,e stroke. Brain injury and ventilator patients could also have upper extremity deficits. Music therapy can provide a fun and motivational atmosphere to the rehabilitation process, while increasing upper extremity strength, coordination, and range of motion.

Before discussing appropriate goals and activities, let's go through some basic vocabulary, ideas, and concepts. *Hemiplegia* refers to a person who has one sided *weakness*. *Hemiparalysis* means the patient has one side that is *paralyzed*. Often a patient's arm has no movement, but has return movement after days or weeks of therapy. Occupational therapists use such things as electrical stimulation, exercise, and ranging the arm to help the patient gain some return of movement. Some patients have "return" and some don't. But it is important to encourage your patients to keep trying because only time and hard work will bring any results.

The following defines terminology you might hear an occupational or physical therapist use:

tone: refers to muscle firmness. Relaxed muscles have small contractions to give firmness to a muscle. These small contractions do not give movement.

hypertonia: increased tone. For instance, an arm becomes perpetually flexed and begins to curl up in front of the chest. The muscles feel hard and almost knotted because it is in a state of constant flexion. This can be extremely painful. Sometimes increased tone can be decreased with muscle relaxors so that an occupational or physical therapist can stretch the extremity. Hypertonia can be described as *spastic* or *rigid.*

hypotonia: decreased tone. Muscles with decreased tone are often called *flaccid*. The muscles lose their shape.

decreased sensation: CVA patients often have decreased sensation and proprioception in their affected side. Decreased sensation can be somewhat dangerous because the patient might cut an arm and not feel it. Often you'll see these patients' arms accidentally pinned between their wheelchair armrest and their bodies, or in some other seemingly uncomfortable or pinched position. If you see this, ask or tell the patients you are going to move their arm and then move it into a better position.

decreased proprioception: often results in patients not knowing where their arm is positioned. A proprioceptor is a sensory receptor in muscles, tendons, joints, and the internal ear. Proprioceptors in effect send messages to the brain to tell the brain where parts of the body are positioned at any given time. They also send messages regarding balance, orientation, awareness of posture, and the knowledge of weight and position of other objects in relation to the patient's body . For instance, if you close your eyes and put your arm in the air, you will still know where your arm is positioned. But a patient with decreased proprioception will not. You may encounter stroke patients who keep asking for someone to go and get their arm out of their room, and patients who were not aware they still had an arm!

Positioning

Let's take a moment to talk briefly about positioning an affected side. Positioning patients in a wheelchair is actually a big issue for therapists, because many CVA, TBI, and ventilator patients have such decreased muscle strength in their bodies they can find themselves in some awkward and harmful positions. For the music therapist, there are a few positioning items to keep in mind while working on upper extremity strength, coordination, and range of motion exercises:

• Never pull on the arm of the affected side, especially if there is no muscle tone to support the shoulder joint. The tendons may stretch and not be able to function as efficiently if the person gets return in that arm.

• Never let the affected arm hang off the side of the wheelchair. Gravity is pulling on that weak arm. The force of gravity plus the weight of the arm can also hurt the shoulder joint and tendons.

• Support a weak or sagging wrist during activities. Patients may not have the ability to hold their wrist up. If you see it sagging, support it with your hand so their tendons don't stretch. Another reason to support the wrist is that it may facilitate their success in completing the task. Supporting the wrist may enable a patient to move the arm forward to reach a drum.

- Watch for swelling in the hand. Though the occupational therapists usually deal with upper extremity swelling, it is always good to keep an eye out for potential problems. If there is swelling in the patient's hand, usually the occupational therapist will administer ice or a massage, or give the patient a glove that provides pressure or a wedge that will keep the hand elevated.

Goals for Patients With Upper Extremity Needs

Appropriate goals for patients with upper extremity needs include but are not limited to:

- Increase upper extremity gross motor and fine motor strength and coordination
- Increase active or passive range of motion
- Provide adaptive equipment for musicians who want to continue to play their instrument

Appropriate Activities and Important Concepts

The following activities can be completed on an individual basis or as a group. In a group setting it might also be appropriate to include patients with little or no return on their affected side. They can follow these activities with their unaffected side or use their unaffected side to physically assist their affected side (passive range of motion).

Drumming

Drumming is a wonderful gross motor activity and can be done with or without a mallet. It requires a controlled up and down movement in a variety of directions, depending upon the angle of the drum. Hold the drum in your lap or in the air at an angle, depending upon the needs of the patient. Having a drum with a handle in the back to hold on to with one of your hands frees your other hand for physical assistance.

Have the patient drum with or without music, depending upon the distractibility and physical abilities of the patient. For instance, if a person has little or slow movements, fast steady music is not appropriate because the patient cannot keep up with the rhythm of the music and therefore simply creates noise. Music should enhance the activity or exercise and should always be used for a reason. Using music in your session should not cause confusion or become a distraction from the goal of the session. Singing improvised lyrics during the drumming activity allows for direction and vocal cueing, as well as adding musical interest.

Having the patient use a mallet to hit the drum requires grasping strength. If the person does not have a tight grip, use an adaptive device to go around the handle so a wider grip is available. A large sponge with a hole in the middle (where the mallet can go through) or an elastic bandage wrapped around the bottom of the mallet handle are two inexpensive ideas for creating an adaptive grip. As the patients' grip improves, they will be able to grasp smaller things.

Conducting

Conducting also requires gross motor movements as well as grasping. It is a great activity that documents progress as well. Have patients hold a marker in the affected hand. Tape a large sheet of paper to the wall about the height of the patient. Draw a large square for 4/4 time, or a triangle for 3/4 time. Play music that is slow to moderate in tempo, depending upon the abilities of each patient. Have them trace the square or triangular lines you have drawn. They can stand or sit during this exercise. Have patients continue the exercise throughout the entire selection of music to increase muscle strength and endurance. Use a different color marker each time and provide a color key for successive sessions on the piece of paper. In this way, patients can see firsthand their progress. This exercise also provides patients with a goal for each session—to consistently draw on the outside of the last trial, thus improving active range of motion and muscle strength.

Autoharp

Strumming an autoharp is a great music task for increasing sitting balance and upper extremity strength, coordination, active range of motion, and fine motor grasping skills. Playing the chords and strumming the autoharp requires upper extremity bilateral coordination because each extremity is performing a completely different task simultaneously.

Begin by having patients take the pick with their affected side. If necessary, use an adaptive gripping device and an extra large pick. While you play the appropriate chords, have patients strum back and forth with the longest strum possible.

If patients can play with both hands, color-code the necessary chords (i.e., tape a small piece of colored construction paper on the chord keys). Then highlight the music with the corresponding colors. Try having patients cross their arms and play a song so that each hand is crossing midline to play chords or strum. For example, if the chords are on the left side and strings on the right side, the left hand would strum while the right hand plays the chords.

Keyboard

Playing the color-coded keyboard provides a fun way to increase fine motor skills, sitting balance, and cognitive skills. It also gives a sense of accomplishment to some patients when they can successfully play a song on the keyboard.

Because many stroke and brain injury patients have never played the keyboard before, you must try to guarantee success. Color-code C through G for the left hand and the right hand. Trace your left and right hand on a piece of paper. On this piece of paper, color code the tips of the fingers on the traced hand corresponding to the colors on the keyboard. For instance, if C is red, then the left pinky and the right thumb would be colored red. Place the traced left or right hand on the music stand for patients to reference. Have patients position the corresponding hand on the corresponding colors. Then point to different fingers, such as the red pinky. Instruct patients to play the notes as you point to them on the traced hand.

As patients becomes skilled at this first step, advance to reading color-coded notes on a page. Have them play with each hand separately, together, and then as a duet where they play with one hand and you play a simple accompaniment. Remember to instruct them to turn on and off the keyboard for problem solving and memory skills.

When color coding a keyboard, keep in mind that stroke and brain injury patients could have had their eyes affected by the accident. They could be easily distracted by too many notes, so draw the notes large and don't place too many on one page. Also remember the patients may not be able to distinguish between some colors, such as red and orange, so avoid placing them right next to each other as much as possible. Yellow can be a difficult color for many people to see. Included in the back of the worksheet section is an example of an original simple color-coded song (pages 114–115).

Shaking Instruments

Rhythm instruments such as maracas, hand bells, and hand chimes all require the fine motor task of grasping and the gross motor task of shaking the instrument to create sound. Play these instruments to popular music and create color-coded tunes for tone chimes.

Hand Jive

Doing "hand jive" motions to music can be a fun way to exercise to music as well. Choose music with a clear, steady beat. Patting knees, clapping, tapping your shoulders, and tapping your head are all good motions to practice. To increase the difficulty, take turns being the leader. When a person leads one motion, have him/her point to another patient to lead the next motion, and so on.

Parachute

Holding on to a parachute with the affected and unaffected sides provides a great muscle strength and range of motion activity. Use slow, relaxing music to create a smooth, flowing motion with the parachute. Upbeat music in a moderate tempo can be used to positively alter the mood. Again, the music should enhance the activity and have a purpose.

Throwing balls on the parachute is another fun twist on this activity. Throw one at a time to prolong the interest. Remember to time and space the intervals on added twists to activities slowly and always monitor the interest level of the group. For example, introduce the parachute. After some of the novelty has worn off (say, 3–5 minutes) add one ball. When the novelty of this has worn off, add another ball, and so on. Small, brightly colored foam balls, as well as small beach balls and balloons work well.

Streamers

Streamer activities are great for using in groups. They focus on fine motor grasping through holding the dowels, and gross motor movements in twirling the streamers. Use fast, upbeat music to increase enjoyment.

As with any group activity, be sure to uphold the group's interest by taking a streamer yourself and walking throughout the group singing and twirling your own streamer with the patients. It is important that no aides, techs, or helpers are on the outside simply watching. They should be participating with a smile on their faces and rhythm in their feet.

Stick Activities

Use sticks while doing imitative movements to music. Develop routines and sequences, and utilize partner activities when appropriate to enhance social interaction.

Music and Movement Groups

Here are some additional activities that are fun and beneficial when conducting a music and movement group. These groups could be a co-treat opportunity for you and an occupational or physical therapist.

Sing along: Use a marker to draw a tic-tac-toe or checkerboard pattern on a posterboard. In the squares write the titles to popular songs. Require the patient to throw a beanbag on to the posterboard to choose the next song.

Playing instruments to popular music: Use maracas, bells, drums, sticks, tone chimes, etc. Ask patients to remember instrument names, song titles, and performers for added cognitive tasks.

Musical clothes: Have a garbage bag (or 2 or 3, depending on the size of the group) filled with oversized clothes. Play music as the bags are passed around. When the music stops, whoever is holding the bag must reach in, pull out an item of clothing, and put it on. The person with the most/least clothes wins. For extra fun, a "fashion show" can be given at the end of the game, with the dressed-up patients rolling or walking down the "runway" modeling their new styles.

Dancing: Patients can dance in their wheelchairs, or stand up and dance with a therapist. Patients in wheelchairs should have a therapist, technician, or another patient to dance with at least some of the time for "freestyle" dancing. To provide more structure, create 16 beats of arm and/or leg choreography to a song and repeat them throughout the song.

Marching or kicking to music: Work those hip flexors and quadriceps used for walking!

Musical Ambulation: Walk in a circle or line to music. This requires a lot of staff providing one-to-one care.

CHAPTER 10

✦✦✦

SITTING BALANCE

General Information

Sitting balance can be a very important issue for stroke, brain injury, ventilator, or any patient who has been bed-ridden for some time. Decreased trunk control results in a person not being able to sit up in a chair. In addition, a person must have sufficient trunk control and strength before he or she can walk.

There are two types of sitting balance: *static* and *dynamic*. *Static* sitting balance refers to a person sitting still on a mat or chair. *Dynamic* sitting balance refers to a person being able to lean forward, left, right, and backward and still be able to pull himself or herself to an upright sitting position. Therapists usually work on static sitting balance before they can work on dynamic sitting balance, because dynamic takes more muscles and is a harder task.

Goals for Patients With Sitting Balance Needs

Appropriate goals for patients with sitting balance needs include but are not limited to:

- Increase static sitting balance
- Increase dynamic sitting balance

Appropriate Activities and Important Concepts

Static Sitting Balance Exercises

Playing the keyboard, autoharp, and many other instruments require good posture and sitting balance. While practicing other areas of deficits, be sure to note a patient's trunk control or sitting balance abilities. Occupational therapists and physical therapists often have these patients simply sitting on a mat. This could be an ideal co-treat situation where you are having patients play instruments while they are sitting with good posture. Be sure to time patients' endurance and ability to maintain trunk control so you can keep data.

Dynamic Sitting Balance Exercises

Anything that requires reaching or moving constitutes a dynamic sitting balance activity. Be sure patients are in a position where their feet are flat on the floor and they can sit up with as little support for their back as possible. Again, this is a wonderful opportunity to co-treat with occupational therapists or physical therapists: they support the patients' posture while you supply the instruments to reach for or hit.

Reaching with a mallet to hit a moving drum and reaching for bells both require dynamic sitting balance. For another variation, place a drum on each side of the patient and have the patient hit the left drum with the right hand and vice versa. This requires crossing the body's midline to hit each drum. A variation of this activity is to use a tamborine or sticks. You can also develop a stick routine.

Leaning forward is also an important motion because one must lean forward to stand up from the wheelchair. By doing this, patients are reaching out of their base of support. Position your knees in front of the patients' knees, with their feet flat on the floor. Place the drum on your knees. Have the patients pat (with both hands if possible) their knees, then lean forward and hit the drum on your knees. Repeat. See if your patients can keep a steady beat.

Once your patients are strong enough and coordinated enough to do this motion to a steady beat, have them play along to recorded music or sing a song to the rhythm.

CHAPTER 11

◆◆◆

LOWER EXTREMITIES

General Information

In the same way an upper extremity becomes weak as the result of a CVA or TBI, the lower extremity of the affected side also becomes weak and/or paralyzed. Movement usually returns in the lower extremity first before the upper extremity, but there may not be any return at all.

Many of the same concerns for the upper extremity apply to the lower extremity. The patient's wheelchair will probably have a leg rest on the affected side so the leg does not drag along the floor while the wheelchair is being pushed. For this reason, it is vital to have the leg on the leg rest before pushing the wheelchair. Depending upon their sensation and proprioception, patients may or may not be able to feel a leg or foot trapped under the wheelchair. Be sure to reference the section on proprioception and sensation in the chapter on upper extremities (page 66).

Music therapists usually work on lower extremities in two areas: strengthening leg muscles, and using music to cue steady gait.

Goals for Patients With Lower Extremity Needs

Appropriate goals for patients with lower extremity needs include but are not limited to:

- Increase weight shift with right/left emphasis
- Increase ability to perform sit-to-stand
- Increase strength and coordination in leg muscles
- Develop or improve walking gait

Appropriate Activities and Important Concepts

Weight Shifting

Weight shifting refers, of course, to shifting your weight or rocking from one side to the other. Weight shifting is useful not only while standing, but also while sitting in a chair and laying down. Weight shifting allows you to change positions while you are sitting, which can be important while doing transfers, personal care and daily living skills, as well as performing the necessary "pressure reliefs" during the day to avoid pressure sores.

Leaning exercises with drums, tambourines, and sticks are useful for weight shifting while in a chair; however, the patient's bottom must be off of the chair or surface. Therefore, the instrument must be placed to the side of patients, so they are not turning or leaning with their trunk, but actually shifting weight onto one hip. Their body should be facing forward, yet they are only sitting on one hip. If the patient is lying down, the same instruments can be used to encourage a patient to shift weight or roll over to one side.

Sit to Stand

To stand up, patients must lean forward ("nose over their knees"), and push up with their arms on their arm rests while using their leg muscles. Songs can be used as a mnemonic device to assist with remembering the steps. This also requires a lot of strength. Choreograph dances that require a patient to stand up, do squats, shift weight (particularly when holding on to a bar for balance), do small kicks, and sit back down. These movements are all helpful for standing up and walking. Sometimes very rhythmic music will help to cue the patient.

Strengthening Exercises

Marching to music is beneficial for patients relearning to walk, because it works the hip flexor muscles, which are necessary for walking. Patients must place both feet flat on the floor. Have them march left and right in their chair to the rhythm of the music. Of course, be sure to pick music with a steady, marching beat and an appropriate tempo. Too easy? Place the feet on something elevated, like a telephone book. The extra height adds difficulty.

Toe raises to music is another good strengthening activity. With feet flat on the floor, raise toes up and down to strengthen the muscles needed for walking. Similarly, raising heels is another beneficial activity for strengthening walking muscles.

Kicking a drum works the quadricep muscles that are also necessary for walking. With the patients' feet flat on the floor, hold a drum up in front of their legs, and have them kick the drum. Again, placing the feet on an elevated level such as a telephone book increases the difficulty of the exercise. It may be necessary to physically assist the affected side by lifting the affected leg slightly right above the knee. This allows patients to bend and straighten their leg more freely.

While patients are sitting in a wheelchair with the brakes off, have them "walk their feet." Moving the wheelchair in this way utilizes the hamstring muscles. This can also be done to music with a steady beat. As always, the music should serve a purpose, such as to cue motion, the speed of the gait, or provide a more enjoyable environment.

Gait Training

Pioneering research conducted at the Robert F. Unkefer Academy of Neurologic Music Therapy, Colorado State University, has contributed to a growing body of research in the area of music and gait training, especially with CVA, TBI, and Parkinson's patients. There are several informative journal and magazine articles regarding this research (e.g., Thaut, McIntosh, Prassa, & Rice, 1993; Thaut, Schleiffers, & Davis, 1991).

The basic concept in gait training involves music as an auditory cue that triggers the muscles to work more efficiently in these populations. Patients who have had uneven stride lengths, shuffling steps, and decreased initiation have improved their gait by listening to and walking with music containing a simple, steady beat. When a quicker tempo is applied, the number of steps per minute increases, thus increasing the gait speed.

More detailed information regarding this subject is provided in a video entitled, *Rhythmic Sensorimotor Music Therapy for Gait Training With Parkinson's Disease Patients* (Thaut, Rice, & McIntosh, 1994).

TIPS FOR THE MUSIC THERAPIST

◆◆◆

➤ Doctors are extremely busy.

➤ Some people will "re-stroke" in the hospital. In other words, they have another stroke soon after their latest one.

➤ Be confident, but not cocky.

➤ Stroke patients' eye prescriptions often change after a stroke. Old glasses may not help much anymore.

➤ An *NG tube* is a tube placed up the nose and down towards the stomach for feeding when a person has poor appetite, and/or temporary (i.e., 2 or 3 weeks) but severe swallowing difficulties.

➤ A *PEG tube* is surgically placed directly into the stomach for long-term (i.e., a few months) nutritional issues or swallowing difficulties.

➤ Don't take it personally if the doctors are hesitant to jump on the "Music Therapy Bandwagon."

➤ A *yonker* is a suctioning device used for trach patients to suction around the external areas of the trach when the patient coughs secretions out of the opening.

➤ Some people are very intelligent. Some just think they are.

➤ Therapy, medications, special beds, etc., all are given only if they have a specific physician's order. However, if a patient has been overlooked for music therapy, go to the doctor to request a *verbal order* and briefly explain why. You may have to write the order yourself on the chart and then place it in a location where the physician knows he or she needs to sign off on the orders. Learn the ropes!

➤ Don't jump to medical conclusions too quickly. You aren't a doctor.

➤ ↑ means "increase," ↓ means "decrease." 2**⊙** means "secondary to." "Pt." is the abbreviation for patient. You can use these shorthand symbols in medical charts; however, most facilities have a listing of approved abbreviations for consistency and clarity of communication.

➤ Collect and know research related to your field.

➤ You can learn a lot from your patients.

➤ Don't take it personally if doctors forget to give you orders for a very appropriate patient.

➤ Before you give patients a drink, ALWAYS find out if they need thickened liquids or have any diet restrictions.

➤ When writing goals on a chart, some common goal words and phrases may be:

increase/decrease	attends to task
range of motion (ROM)	cognitive skills/abilities
communication skills	reading and writing tasks
cognitive skills	to facilitate
upper extremity (UE) activities	lower extremity (LE) activities

➤ When writing a goal in a chart, "increase" or "decrease" a symptom or an ability, not a diagnosis. For example, you cannot "decrease a stroke," "decrease aphasia," "decrease dysarthria," or "decrease paralysis."

➤ A patient's prognosis is never certain: everyone needs to try his or her best. Avoid being negative or too positive in front of patients and/or their families.

➤ When writing goals on a medical chart, you may have to specify that your goals are being completed "during music therapy." For instance; "Pt. will complete 1-step commands with 50% accuracy *during music therapy*." This is because insurance does not want to pay for "duplication of services." If speech therapy measures 1-step commands, why should MT? "During music therapy" specifies that you are implementing this task from a music therapy angle.

➢ Learn the doctors' personalities. Some are very particular about staying in power. Others welcome your initiative.

➢ Always listen to others. Then silently decide if you agree.

➢ Don't be too disappointed if the doctors don't take the time to learn about all of the wonderful research in the music therapy field. But have research ready in case they ask questions.

➢ Feeling unsure about the music therapy benefits? Read some research. Then revamp your program if necessary.

➢ Be prepared for a variety of unofficial job titles, such as "The Music Lady/Man," "The Music Teacher," "The Guitar Picker," and "The Traveling Minstrel," to name a few.

➢ You aren't expected to know everything. Especially the first month.

➢ Good words to describe progress include "displays" and "exhibits" (i.e., patient exhibits mild confusion, or patient exhibits socially inappropriate behavior).

➢ Ice melts in thickened liquids and makes them thin.

➢ Before giving diabetic patients food or drinks, make sure they may have the item in question.

➢ Ear, Nose, and Throat (ENT) doctors diagnose paralyzed vocal cords and vocal cord nodules. Speech therapists are not supposed to treat for paralyzed vocal cords without a diagnosis because it could harm the patient's voice.

➢ Use the "cueing hierarchy":
    1. State task
    2. Verbal cueing ("you hit the_____" or "you hit the dr__")
    3. Imitative cueing
    4. Physical assistance

➢ Smile! Even when you don't feel like it.

Quick Tips for Running Successful Groups

➤ Groups should always be in a circle if possible.

➤ The music therapist should ALWAYS be moving and interacting with the group. Interaction includes singing to, playing with, dancing with, smiling, eye contact, and/or winking at patients.

➤ Be sure everyone can participate and feels included.

➤ Be sure there are enough instruments, parachute space, space to move, etc., for everyone.

➤ Provide adaptive equipment, words to songs, and previously adapted instruments; have all of the instruments ready to go!

➤ Have aides, techs, and helpers to assist individuals. They should be active participants, not conspicuous observers.

➤ HAVE YOUR MUSIC CUED AND READY . . . nothing loses attention like rewinding a tape or looking for a CD.

➤ Speak loudly and enunciate all instructions and explanations clearly.

➤ Nobody should talk during the music—this includes you and your instructions and directions!

➤ SMILE!!

MUSIC THERAPY DATA SHEET

✦✦✦

Patient _____

Week of _____

Music Therapy Data Sheet

Targeted Goals	Monday	Tuesday	Wednesday	Thursday	Friday

WORKSHEETS

✦✦✦

Name_____   **Date**_____

Music Therapy
Tracing/Copying Shapes

Trace and/or copy these shapes.

Name_____   **Date**_____

Music Therapy
Tracing Notes on the Staff

Trace over the lines to draw music notes.

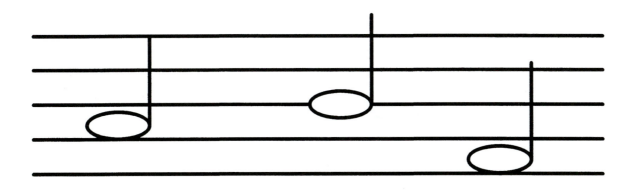

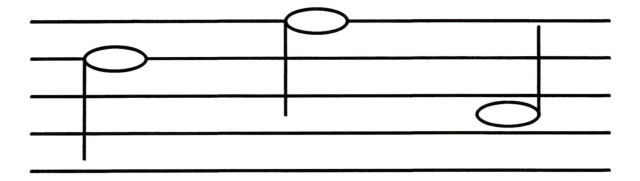

Developed by Elizabeth H. Wong, MT-BC   Writing Skills

Name_____   **Date**_____

Music Therapy: Tracing Notes (II)

Trace over the dotted lines to draw music notes.

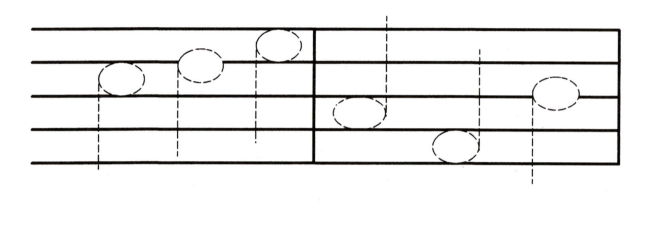

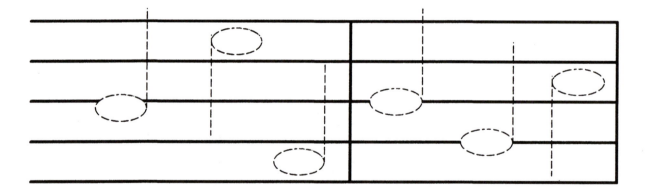

Developed by Elizabeth H. Wong, MT-BC   Writing Skills

Name_____ Date_____

Music Therapy

Trace the following words

1. d r u m

2. p i a n o

3. b e l l s

4. g u i t a r

5. k e y b o a r d

Name

Date

Music Therapy

Cross out the black music notes.

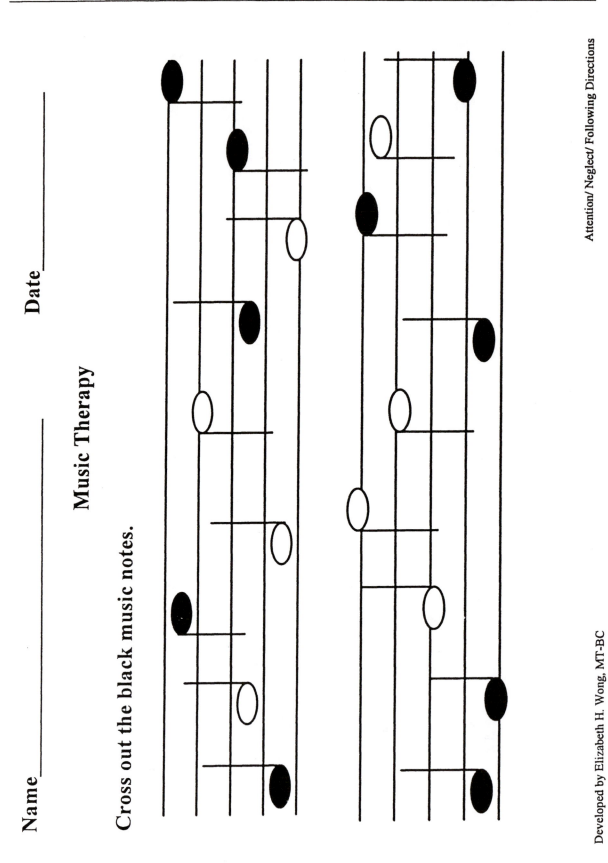

Developed by Elizabeth H. Wong, MT-BC

Name_____   **Date**_____

Music Therapy

Draw a line from the picture on the left to the matching picture on the right.

Name_____   Date_____

Music Therapy

Draw a line from the word on the left to the matching word on the right.

1. bells	guitar
2. guitar	drum
3. piano	keyboard
4. drum	bells
5. keyboard	maracas
7. maracas	piano
8. rainstick	rainstick

Developed by Elizabeth H. Wong, MT-BC   Identifying/Matching

Name:_____ **Date**_____

Music Therapy
Copying Music Notes

Directions: Copy these notes on the lines below.

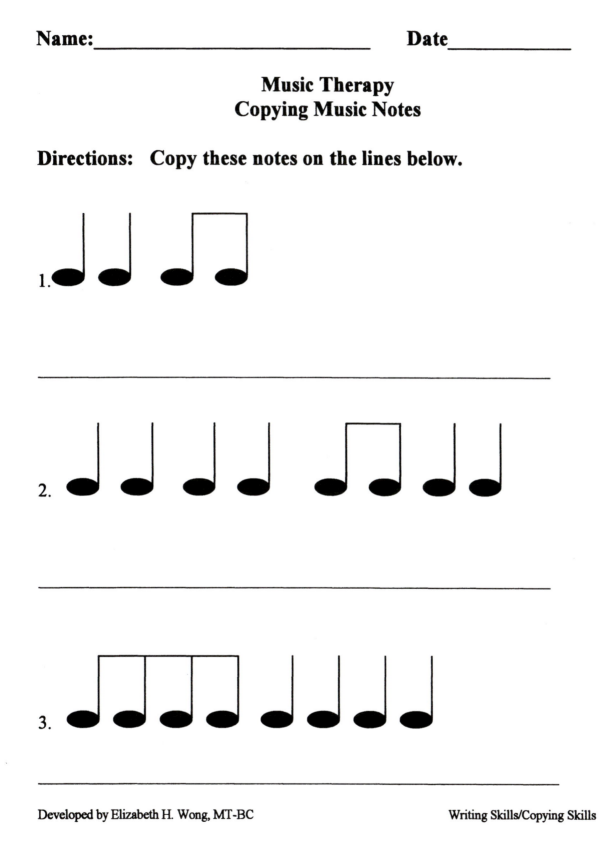

Name_____   **Date**_____

Music Therapy
Copying Music Notes of the Staff (I)

Place the notes in the correct line or space on the music staff.

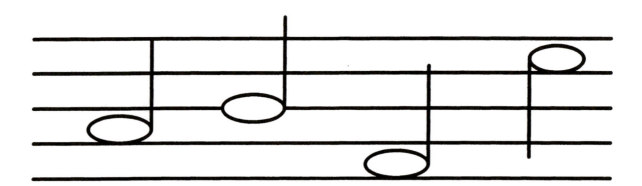

Name_____   **Date**_____

Music Therapy
Copying Music Notes on the Staff (II)

Place the notes in the correct line or space on the music staff.

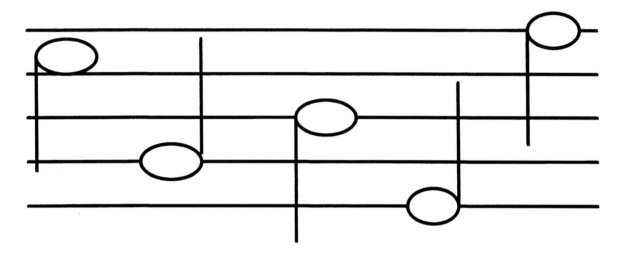

Name_____ **Date**_____

Music Therapy
Copying Words

Copy the following words.

1. b e l l _____

2. p i a n o_____

3. g u i t a r_____

4. d r u m _____

5. m u s i c _____

6. s o n g s _____

Name_____ **Date**_____

Music Therapy
Copying Words

Copy these words:

1. drum_____

2. bells_____

3. guitar_____

4. keyboard_____

5. rainstick_____

6. maracas_____

7. piano_____

8. harp_____

9. violin_____

10. flute_____

Name_____   **Date**_____

Music Therapy
Copying Sentences

Copy these sentences.

1. Hit the drum.

_____

2. Ring the red bell.

_____

3. Shake the maracas.

_____

4. Where is your harmonica?

_____

5. Who wants to sing first?

_____

6. He plays the guitar with his friends.

_____

7. She knows the words to that song.

_____

Name_____ **Date**_____

Music Therapy
Copying Sentences

Copy these sentences.

1. Hit the drum with me.

_____

2. Please ring the purple bell.

_____

3. Shake the brown maracas.

_____

4. John lost the music.

_____

5. Who wants to play the keyboard?

_____

6. He plays the drum with the band.

_____

Developed by Elizabeth H. Wong, MT-BC   Writing Skills

Name_____   **Date**_____

Music Therapy
Spelling Practice

Fill in the missing vowels (a e i o u).

1. d r __ m

2. b __ l l s

3. m __ s i c

4. p __ a n o

5. s __ n g

6. k __ y b o __ r d

7. d __ n c e

8. g u __ t a r

9. "O h S u s __ n n a"

10. "A m a z __ n g G r __ c e"

Developed by Elizabeth H. Wong, MT-BC   Writing Skills/Problem Solving

Name_____   **Date**_____

Music Therapy
Spelling Practice (II)

Fill in the missing vowels (a e i o u).

1. Hit   the   dr__m.

2. Pl__y   the   guit__r.

3. Turn   __n   the   k__ybo__rd.

4. S__ng   th__   song.

5. She   pl__ys   th__   guitar   v__ry   w__ll.

6. Wh__t   kind of   m__sic   do   you   lik__?

7. D__   y__u   lik__   "Am__z__ng   Gr__ce"?

8. He   d__nces   to   th__   mus__c.

9. Can   they   pl__y   th__   dr__ms?

10. Wh__re   is   the   r__dio?

Developed by Elizabeth H. Wong, MT-BC   Writing Skills/Problem Solving

Name_____   **Date**_____

Music Therapy
Spelling Practice (III)

Fill in the missing vowels (a e i o u).

1. H__t   th __   dr__m.

2. Sh__k__   th__   b __lls.

3. Pl__y   th__   k__yb__ __rd.

4. R__ng   th__   gre __ n   b __ ll.

5. Wh__t   d__   y__u   w__nt   t__   s__ng?

6. D__   y__u   lik__   "Am__z__ng   Gr__ce"?

7. Sh__   pl__ys   th__   a__toharp   v__ry   w__ll.

8. He   d__nces   t__   th__   m__s__c.

9. C__n   th__y   pl__y   th__   dr__ms?

10. Wh__t   kind   __f   mus__c   do   yo __
    list__ n   t __?

Developed by Elizabeth H. Wong, MT-BC   Writing Skills/Problem Solving

Name_____   **Date**_____

Music Therapy
Following Written Directions (I)

Follow the directions.

1. **Draw a line.**

2. **Draw a circle.**

3. **Draw an X.**

4. **Draw a square.**

5. **Draw the letter "s".**

6. **Circle the word "harmonica".**

    harmonica

7. **Cross out the word "piano"**

    piano

8. **Underline the word "guitar".**

    guitar

9. **Draw a square around the word "dance".**   **dance**

10. **Circle the word "keyboard".**   **keyboard**

Developed by Elizabeth H. Wong, MT-BC   Writing Skills/Problem Solving

Name_____ Date_____

Music Therapy
Following Written Directions (II)

Follow the directions.

1. Draw a circle around the word "music."   music

2. Underline the word "trumpet."   trumpet

3. Cross out the word "country."   country music

4. Draw a square around the word "danced."   She danced.

5. Underline the word "guitar" in the following sentence.

    Jerry played the guitar.

6. Underline the word "harmonica" in the following sentence.

    Susie plays the harmonica.

7. Circle the word "piano" in the following sentence.

    The piano was out of tune.

8. Circle the word "radio."

    The kids played the radio too loud.

9. Draw a square around the word "saxophone."

    The jazz players loved the sound of his saxophone.

Name_____   **Date**_____

Music Therapy
Following Written Directions (III)

Follow the directions.

1. Underline the word "music" in the following sentence.

   The little girl loved to sing to the music.

2. Circle the word "flute" in this sentence.

   How could he play the flute so well?

3. Cross out the word "country" in this sentence.

   The band played country music all night long.

4. Cross out the "a" in the following word.   d a n c e

5. Cross out the "s" in the following word.   s i n g

6. Cross out every "t" in the following word.   t r u m p e t

6. Underline every "o" in the following sentence.

   J o h n   p l a y s   t h e   s o n g   v e r y   s l o w l y.

7. Underline every "i" in the following sentence.

   H i s   p i a n o   w a s   i n   h i s   g r a n d m o t h e r ' s   h o u s e.

Developed by Elizabeth H. Wong, MT-BC   Writing Skills/Problem Solving

Name _____   **Date**_____

Music Therapy
Song Lyric Analysis

<u>Baa Baa Black Sheep</u>

Baa Baa Black Sheep have you any wool?
"Yes, sir. Yes, sir. Three bags full.
One for my master, one for my dame,
one for the little boy who lives in the lane."
Baa Baa Black Sheep have you any wool?
"Yes, sir.   Yes, sir. Three bags full."

1. What is the name of this song?_____

_____

2. How many bags did he have?_____

_____

3. What is in the bags?_____

4. Who lives in the lane?_____

_____

5. Who are the bags for?_____

_____

6. What can you make out of wool?_____

Developed by Elizabeth H. Wong, MT-BC   SCORE_____

Name_____ **Date**_____

Music Therapy
Song Lyric Analysis

Read and sing the song. Answer the questions below.

<u>Oh Susanna</u>

**Oh I come from Alabama with a banjo on my knee.
I'm going to Louisiana for my true love for to see.**

**Oh Susanna, don't you cry for me.
I come from Alabama with a banjo on my knee.**

1. What is the name of this song?_____

_____

2. Where is he going? _____

3. Why is he going there?_____

_____

4. What instrument is on his knee?_____

5. Where does he come from?_____

Developed by Elizabeth H. Wong, MT-BC   SCORE_____

Name_____   **Date** _____

MUSIC THERAPY
SYMBOL SUBSTITUTION

These are the notes of the staff.

F   A   C   E

Draw the notes for the following letters:

A   C   E

C   A   F   E

Developed by Elizabeth H. Wong, MT-BC   Attention/Spatial Perception/Sequential Thinking

Name_____   **Date _____**

MUSIC THERAPY
SYMBOL SUBSTITUTION

These are the notes in the spaces of the staff.

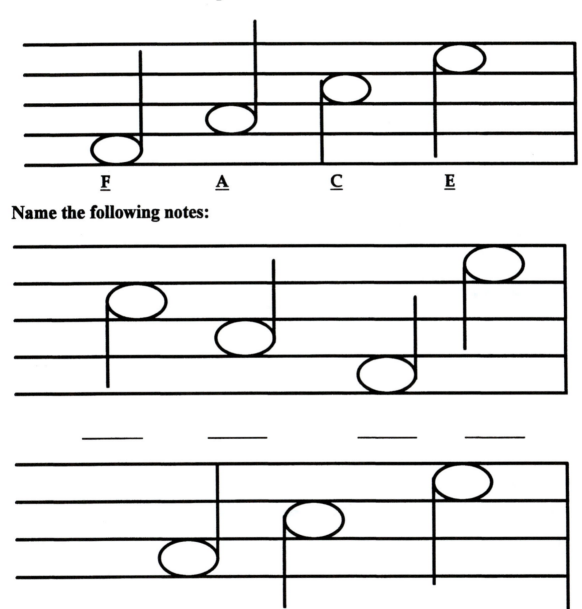

Name the following notes:

Name_____ **Date**_____

Music Therapy
Word Scramble (I)

Unscramble the following words:

1. lebls   _____

2. ipona   _____

3. mrud   _____

4. ratgui   _____

5. dario   _____

6. msicu   _____

7. lutef   _____
****

Words to choose from:

radio   **music**   **flute**
bells   **piano**   **guitar**   **drum**

Developed by Elizabeth H. Wong, MT-BC   Writing Skills/Problem Solving

Name_____ **Date**_____

Music Therapy
Word Scramble (II)

Unscramble the following words:

1. nedac   _____

2. usimc   _____

3. turmtep   _____

4. jobna   _____

5. casyblm   _____

6. dario   _____

7. phsxanoe   _____

****

Words to choose from:

trumpet   banjo   saxophone
cymbals   music   dance
radio

Developed by Elizabeth H. Wong, MT-BC   Writing Skills/Problem Solving

Name_____ **Date**_____

Music Therapy
Word Scramble (III)

Unscramble the following words:

1. lebls   _____

2. ipona   _____

3. mrud   _____

4. ratgui   _____

5. raascam   _____

6. dario   _____

7. bordakye   _____

8. msicu   _____

9. lutef   _____

10. viilon   _____

Name_____   **Date**_____

Music Therapy
Convergent Inferences

Using the following descriptions, name the object or action.

1. This instrument is made of wood and has six strings. It sits on your knee or hangs from a neck strap. You can strum it or pick it.

_____

2. This instrument has black and white keys. You sit on a bench and press the keys with your fingers to play it. It has three pedals close to the floor.

_____

3. This object is something that plays music. You turn it on and tune into a channel so you can listen to music or people talking.

_____

4. This instrument you hit to make a sound. It keeps the rhythm of the music.

_____

5. This word means moving your body to the music.

_____

6. This is when you use your voice to create music.

_____

7. This instrument has strings and you use a bow to glide across the strings to make sound. You hold this instrument under your chin, hold the bow with one hand, and use your other hand to create the notes on the neck of the instrument.

_____

Developed by Elizabeth H. Wong, MT-BC   Writing Skills/Problem Solving

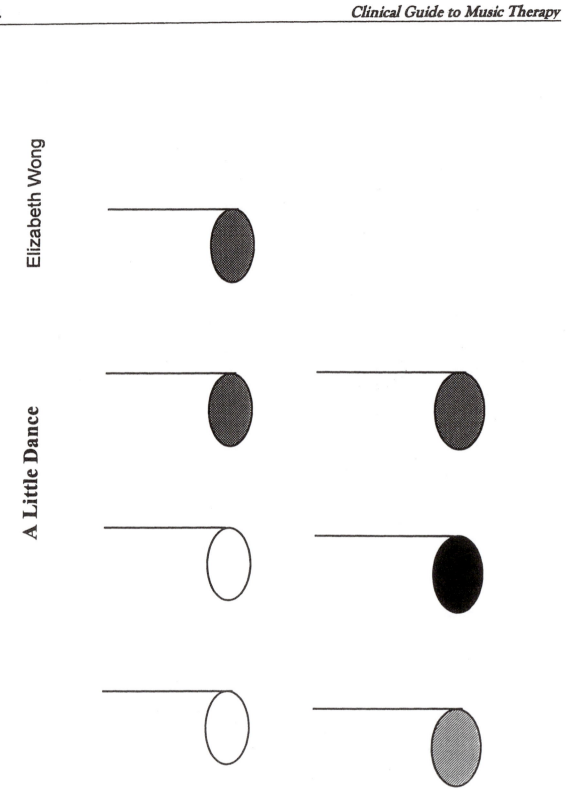

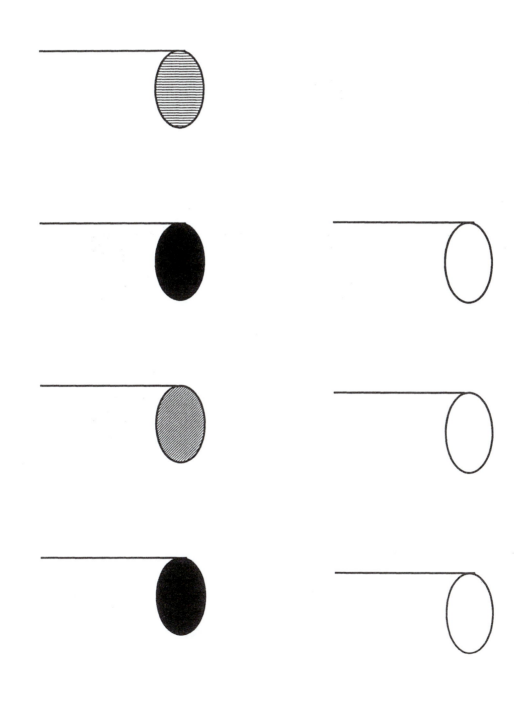

GLOSSARY

♦♦♦

Abcess A collection of pus in a confined area.

Aneurysm An enlargement of a blood vessel caused by a weakening of its wall.

Anopsia A visual deficit; also called a visual field cut (Burlingame & Skalko, 1997). Hemianopsia refers to visual deficits in half of the visual field. For instance, hemianopsia may affect the left side in both eyes. Hemianopsia affects the person's ability to read or scan music, keys on a keyboard, food on their plate, etc.

Anoxia An oxygen deficiency. Anoxia may result in cognitive deficits.

Agnosia The decreased ability to identify familiar objects or persons. It may affect any of the five senses: auditory, visual, olfactory, tactile, or gustatory (Tortora & Grabowski, 1993).

Aphasia The decreased ability to speak or understand words or written language. There are different kinds:

fluent aphasia refers to speech which is fluent but contains paraphasic areas, such as word or sound substitutions. Reading comprehension and writing are also impaired.

nonfluent aphasia refers to speech in which auditory comprehension is better than verbal expression. Reading comprehension is better than written expression (Chapey, 1994).

Apraxia Found in motor movements and physical activities as well as speech, the inability to complete purposeful motor tasks due to uncoordination of muscles. The signals in the brain that would instruct muscles how to perform a task are damaged. Therefore the person cannot physically coordinate those muscles to perform the simple task correctly.

Atherosclerosis Results from a build-up of fatty plaque in the blood vessels. This makes the blood vessels more vulnerable to clotting.

Ataxia Movements that are uncoordinated and jerky. A lack of precision with muscular coordination.

Broca's Area The area of the brain responsible for motor movements used in speech. It is involved in the translation of thoughts into speech (Chapey, 1994).

Catheter A urethral catheter is a tubing device inserted in the bladder that allows the bladder to empty through a tube. The most common type of indwelling catheter is a Foley catheter, which has a receptacle to hold the urine. Because it is gravity driven, the catheter bag should always be below the bladder and there should be no loops in the tubing. Therapists should watch restless patients, as some will pull on their catheter tube (Burlingame & Skalko, 1997).

Clonus Rhythmic moving of an extremity due to muscle tone. Placing weight or moving the extremity usually causes the extremity to stop shaking.

Closed Head Injury These tend to produce diffuse damage and therefore more generalized deficits. The majority of head injuries are closed.

Contusion Regarding head injuries, a jarring of the brain with significant force.

Contracture A shortening or tightening of muscle tissue; an abnormal formation of tissue that prevents a normal range of motion or mobility

Convergent Naming To apply specific items or objects to a group or category. For instance, red, blue, and green are all _____.

CVA Refers to a cerebrovascular accident or a stroke. There are two main types of strokes: *ischemic* is the most common type of stroke. It is caused by a decreased blood supply. *hemorrhagic* is due to a blood vessel that ruptures in the brain.

Divergent Naming To determine which items will fall within a category. For example, the therapist would say, "Name three types of music," to which the answer might be *country*, *classical*, and *rock and roll*.

EEG An electroencephalogram measures brain wave activity. Certain wave patterns may detect brain damage, seizure activity, seizure disorders such as epilepsy, degenerative diseases, and unconsciousness or confusion (Tortora & Grabowski, 1993).

EKG An electrocardiogram measures electrical activity in the heart.

Embolus A thrombus (or clot) that has become dislodged and is carried through the blood stream. If it occurs in an artery, it may stop the flow of blood to a vital organ.

Endotracheostomy A tube placed through the mouth and down the windpipe to facilitate breathing. Only used for up to 2 weeks, although after only a few days complications can occur. If the patient continues to require assistance with respiration, a tracheostomy is done.

EMG Electromyography measures electrical activity of resting and contracting muscles to determine causes of muscular weakness, lack of coordination, paralysis, etc.

Hemorrhage The act of bleeding.

Hematoma A collection of blood, usually resulting from penetrating wounds or blood vessels that rupture.

Hemianopsia See *anopsia*

Hemiparesis Paralysis on one side of the body.

Hemiplegia Weakness on one side of the body.

Increased Intracranial Pressure After a brain injury, there is often a build-up of pressure within the skull, which compresses delicate brain tissue and may lead to further brain injury. The brain, its membranes, and cerebrospinal fluid are all enclosed in the skull. As a result, there is no space to accommodate the accumulation of blood or swelling, which builds pressure (Florida Institute of Neurologic Rehab).

Intracranial Hemorrhage Bleeding into the cranium.

Intracerebral Hemorrhage Bleeding into the brain from a ruptured vessel, which can cause a stroke.

Intracerebral Hematoma A pool of blood collecting within the brain. More specifically, bleeding in and around brain tissue, which leads to a build-up of blood within the brain (Burlingame & Skalko, 1997).

Intubate To insert a tube into a part of the body, such as a trach.

Laceration A cutting of tissue.

MRI Magnetic Resonance Imaging testing. Detects damaged or abnormal soft tissue.

MVA Motor Vehicle Accident.

Neglect (Right/Left) refers to a patient essentially ignoring their affected side. For instance, right-brained stroke patients may have their neck twisted to the right side because their left side is affected. They have left neglect. They may have poor proprioception in the left arm, run into the wall on their left side, eat things only on the right side of their plate, and start reading in the middle of a page.

NPO Stands for nothing by mouth, i.e., food, water, medicine, etc.

Occlusion The closing off of a blood vessel.

Open Head Injury A head injury in which the scalp and skull are penetrated by an object, such as a bullet. These tend to produce more localized damage to the brain.

Proprioception The sense that helps patients know their orientation, positioning, equilibrium, or pressure. A proprioceptor is a sensory receptor located in muscles, joints, tendons, and the internal ear (Burlingame & Skalko, 1997). Decreased proprioception means patients may not realize where their arm is located, or if they still have an arm!

Problem Solving The process of reaching a desired goal. Some skills include: the ability to identify the desired outcome, the ability to gather and choose from relevant information to reach a preferred outcome, anticipating feasible outcomes caused by possible solutions, and selecting the steps which would lead to the desired outcome (Burlingame & Skalko, 1997).

Subarachnoid Hemorrhage The blood from a ruptured blood vessel spreads over the surface of the brain. The most common cause is a ruptured aneurysm (Florida Institute of Neurologic Rehab).

Subdural Hematoma Blood collected between the brain and the *dura*, the membrane that covers the brain and the brain tissue. If this bleeding occurs quickly it is called an acute subdural hematoma. If it occurs slowly over weeks it is called a chronic subdural hematoma (Burlingame & Skalko, 1997).

Subluxation A partial or incomplete dislocation, i.e., in the shoulder joint. Pulling on a flaccid arm can result in a subluxed shoulder because the tendons cannot keep it in place. This can be extremely painful.

Thrombus A clot in an artery.

Thrombosis Clotting in an unbroken blood vessel.

Tracheostomy An opening between the second and fourth tracheal rings into the trachea. A tracheostomy tube is surgically placed in the patient to facilitate breathing. When the "trach" is pulled, the patient is left with the hole, or *stoma*, to close naturally (Burlingame & Skalko, 1997).

Wernicke's Area The area of the brain responsible for auditory association. It determines whether a sound is music, speech, or noise. It also interprets the meaning of speech by translating words into thoughts (Chapey, 1994).

BIBLIOGRAPHY

✦✦✦

ABR and ENG testing. Available: http://www.centreforhearing.com/abr_eng.htm/

ABR versus OAE: Two similar hearing tests. Available: http://deafness.about.com/cs/audiograms/a/abroae.htm/

Ansell, B. J., Keenan, J. E., & de la Rocha, O. (1989). *Western Neuro Sensory Stimulation Profile.* Barbara J. Ansell and Western Neuro Care Center, Inc.

Argyris, S. P. (1994). *The Glasgow Coma Scale.* San Antonio, TX: Communication Skill Builders, Inc.

Bontke, C. F. (Ed.). (1992). Sensory stimulation: Accepted practice or expected practice? *The Journal of Head Trauma Rehabilitation, 7*(4), 115–120.

Burlingame, J., & Skalko, T. K. (1997). *Idyll Arbor's glossary for therapists,* Ravensdale, WA: Idyll Arbor.

Chapey, R. (Ed.). (1994). *Language intervention strategies in adult aphasia.* Baltimore: Williams & Wilkins.

Cofrancesco, E. (1985). The effect of music therapy on hand grasp strength and functional task performance in stroke patients. *Journal of Music Therapy, 22,* 129–145.

Cohen, N. S. (1992). The effect of singing instruction on the speech production of neurologically impaired persons. *Journal of Music Therapy, 29,* 87–102.

Cohen, N. S. (1993). The application of singing and rhythmic instruction as a therapeutic intervention for persons with neurogenic communication disorders. *Journal of Music Therapy, 30,* 81–99.

Cohen, N. S., & Ford, J. (1991). The effect of musical cues on nonpurposeful speech in people with aphasia. *Journal of Music Therapy, 22,* 46–57.

Colan, B. J. (1998, March 9). Moving with the music. *Advance for Physical Therapists.*

Florida Institute of Neurologic Rehab, Inc. *Glossary of terms.* Available: http://www.finr.com/glossary.html#n/

Gervin, A. P. (1991). Music therapy compensatory technique utilizing song lyrics during dressing to promote independence in the patient with a brain injury. *Music Therapy Perspectives, 9,* 87–90.

Hagen, C., Malkmus, D., & Durham, P. (1972). *Levels of cognitive functioning.* Downey, CA: Professional Staff Association of Ranchos Los Amigos Hospital, Inc.

Hurt, C. P., Rice, R. R., McIntosh, G. C., & Thaut, M. H., (1998). Rhythmic auditory stimulation in gait training for patients with traumatic brain injury. *Journal of Music Therapy, 35,* 228–241.

Managing communication and swallowing impairments in tracheostomized and ventilator-dependent adults (1998, September 17). ASHA/RTN Self-Study Satellite Broadcast. Marta Kazandjian, MA, CCC-SLP and Karen Dikeman, MA, CCC-SLP.

Senelick, R. C., & Ryan, C. E., (1998). *Living with brain injury: A guide for families.* Birmingham, AL: HealthSouth Press.

Stach, B. A. (2002). Introduction. In J. Katz (Eds.), *Handbook of clinical audiology.* Philadelphia: Lippincott Williams & Wilkins.

Staum, M. J. (1983). Music and music stimuli in the rehabilitation of gait disorders. *Journal of Music Therapy, 20,* 69–87.

Taylor, D. B. (1997). *Biomedical foundations of music as therapy.* St. Louis, MO: MMB Music.

Thaut, M. H., McIntosh, G. C., Prassa, S. G., & Rice, R. R. (1993). Effect of rhythmic auditory cueing on temporal stride parameters and EMG patterns in hemiparetic gait of stroke patients. *Journal of Neuro Rehabilitation, 7,* 7–16.

Thaut, M., Rice, R. R., & McIntosh, G. C. (1994). *Rhythmic sensorimotor music therapy for gait training with Parkinson's disease patients* [Video]. St. Louis, MO: MMB Music.

Thaut, M., Schleiffers, S., & Davis, W. (1991). The analysis of EMG activity in biceps and triceps muscle in an upper extremity gross motor task under the influence of auditory rhythm. *Journal of Music Therapy, 28*, 64–88.

Tortora, G. J., & Grabowski, S. R. (1993). *Principles of anatomy and physiology* (7th ed.). New York: HarperCollins College Publishers.

Venes, D. (1997). *Taber's cycolpedic medical dictionary.* Philadelphia: F.A. Davis.

What is auditory brainstem response? Available: http://www.vmmc.org/dbNeurophysiology/sec1819.htm/